Even God Had Bad Parenting Days

ancient Jewish wisdom for new parents

Alicia Jo Rabins

BEHRMAN HOUSE
www.behrmanhouse.com

Published by Behrman House, Inc.
Millburn, New Jersey 07041

www.behrmanhouse.com

ISBN 978-1-68115-071-0

Copyright © 2022 by Alicia Jo Rabins

All rights reserved. No part of this publication may be translated, reproduced, stored in a retrieval system or transmitted, in any form or by any means, electronic, mechanical, photocopying, recording or otherwise, for any purpose, without express written permission from the publishers.

Cover image courtesy of Shutterstock/alanadesign.

Library of Congress Control Number: 2022933721

Design by Zahava Bogner
Edited by Tzivia MacLeod and Dena Neusner

Printed in the United States of America

9 8 7 6 5 4 3 2 1

for Sylvia and Elijah,
who made me a mother

Contents

Part 3: The Everyday Sacred: Parenting as *Tikun* 81

Part 4: Parenting as Spiritual Practice: God, the Imperfect Parent 127

Part 5: Moving On: Every Ending Contains a Beginning 189

Preface

C onfession: I'm not a big fan of most parenting books. At least not the ones that pretend to have all the answers.

Being a parent isn't like learning to drive, or training for a competition, or going to school. There's no outside assessment, no finish line, no tests to pass—except the test of waking up each morning and starting over again, together. It's a profoundly intimate, personal experience, and there's no right way to do it, as long as everyone involved is safe, nurtured, and respected.

In other words . . . it's a spiritual practice. And that's why I wanted to write this book.

While I'm decidedly *not* a parenting expert—a fact my kids will be happy to confirm for you—I *am* a teacher of Jewish texts, traditions, and spirituality, as well as a musician and performer creating work that often investigates these texts and traditions. I'm fascinated by how our ancient stories, rituals, and wisdom texts can support us through life's inevitable difficulties. I love how they reframe our individual challenges as an essential part of being human rather than some personal shortcoming.

And when I became a mother, I found that the Jewish texts and traditions I'd been teaching for so long became newly precious to me.

Though I wanted to be a parent with every fiber of my being, those early months and years contained such surprising layers of loss and discomfort amid the profound, earth-shattering joy that I often had trouble even figuring out what I was feeling.

In that confusing place, I found that our traditions—from family stories to mystical creation myths, from holiday rituals to rabbinic concepts—took on a new urgency. They supported me as never before, and I also began to understand them in a new way.

Over and over, they reminded me that I wasn't alone. The Torah is full of stories about people who are just like us: doing their best, muddling through, making mistakes, getting overwhelmed, apologizing, starting over again, keeping going. In my own messy transition to motherhood, I was grateful for their company.

The rituals and traditions of Judaism, both old and new, comforted me as well. I had long appreciated the way Jewish ritual marks the passage of time; during pregnancy, birth, and early motherhood, I felt this even more deeply.

At the end of each week, no matter what had happened in the six days before, there was Shabbat: challah, grape juice, and a moment of quiet and peace in the light of the candles, however brief. Through the year, holidays carried their own gentle reminders too: there is liberation from the narrow places, and sometimes we have to free ourselves (Passover); we can make mistakes, apologize, and move on (Yom Kippur); it's fun to build forts outside that are big enough to sleep in (Sukkot).

On particularly rough days, when I was convinced something must be wrong with me, I thought back to the expression used by the rabbis of the Talmud, *tza'ar gidul banim*, literally, "the pain of raising children." This simple phrase helped me remember that it was, in fact, completely normal to feel like parenting was really, really hard.

So, yeah. You'll notice that this book leans just a little more into the hard parts of parenting, because those were the moments when I needed more support, when I was most grateful to see my own experience reflected in the texts.

But of course, there is so much joy in this journey, and Jewish rituals supported me during those sweet, glowing days of early parenthood too. In simple moments like taking the first bite of warm challah or quietly singing the bedtime Shema to my little one before turning out the light, I felt like I was standing with millions and millions of ancestors who have walked this same path. I doubt those ancestors knew what they were doing as parents any more than I do—but these traditions held them too.

Early parenthood pushes many of us to our limits, physically and emotionally. It's also a magical blessing, a front-row seat to the great mysteries of human existence, of Creation, and of the Divine, whatever we understand that to mean. This is a book about where those two truths intersect, in a place beyond language.

As the Hebrew saying goes, *gam zeh ya'avor*, "this too shall pass," both the difficulty and the sweetness. Growing, birthing, and raising small humans is wild, sacred work. And though it's extremely lonely sometimes, we're not actually alone.

We are held in the light of our traditions, by the gloriously diverse community of Jewish families that stretches back thousands of years. Many generations of ancestors have passed these treasures down, all the way to us. Now they're ours—for us to lean on, to explore, to argue with, to pass down to our own children.

A Note about Language

B ecoming a parent is an experience beyond words, yet writing about it is firmly limited by the capacity of language. So, a few words about the words in this book.

First, *God*.

The most sacred name for God in Judaism is actually unpronounceable, as if to say that we each have to find our own way of interacting with what's beyond us. You are, of course, welcome to translate *God* into your own preferred language: "Nature," "Goddess," "Shechinah," "Spirit," "Creator," any other name, or no name at all. In these pages, I sometimes write about the mystical and ineffable Divine, sometimes (as in the title) about the quasi-literary character of God as described in our sacred books. Take what works for you, and leave the rest.

Then there's the word for *us*, by which I mean, adults in charge of small beings.

As a mother myself, I often use the word *mother* in this book. But I am writing for anyone caring for a child, or thinking about becoming a parent—whatever your gender or age, whether or not you're Jewish, whatever your kids call you. So please know that when I write *mother, mom,* or *mama,* I really mean "parent." And by *parent,* I really mean anyone whose heart and body are pushed to the breaking point with love—and with the sacred, arduous work of caretaking a young human.

PART 1

In the Beginning

Let There Be Mama

1
The Pain of Raising Children

To my daughter, it's just a silly story. But I hope on some
level she understands the story's deeper meaning: we're
here for her, no matter what.

O ver baked pasta casserole last night, I told my kids I was
writing a book about being a mom. "Any stories you want
me to include?" I asked them, as my husband, Aaron, doled out
baby carrots.

Elijah, age three, just wanted to make sure he was in the
book. Sylvia, big sister that she is, yelled out exactly what to
include: "The time I threw up in Dad's lap!"

We all turned to look at Aaron, who nodded, deadpan. "I've
always wanted to be famous for a lapful of puke."

So here's the story of how Aaron had the most uncomfortable
flight of his life, followed by some very rude side-eye from a random
stranger.

We were making the long plane journey back home after
visiting my parents on the East Coast. Elijah didn't exist yet;
Sylvia was a feisty one-year-old. My own body never made enough
milk for her, no matter how hard I tried, so on previous flights,
we'd had to carry drippy, premixed bottles of formula onto the
plane. Now Sylvia was ready for cow's milk; how miraculous to
simply buy it for her at the airport deli before boarding!

On board, I filled a bottle with milk; Sylvia loved it. We were
delayed on the tarmac, but nestled in Aaron's lap, she happily
drained a whole bottle. When the pilot announced we were

cleared for departure, I refilled her bottle, since drinking during takeoff was supposed to keep her ears from hurting.

As we lifted off, Sylvia chugged the second bottle. She grinned and drank and grinned and drank. Then she turned, smiled broadly at Aaron, paused for a moment, and threw up sixteen ounces of milk right into his lap.

She wasn't sick; she had just, shall we say, overindulged.

We looked at the pool of milk, already soaking into his pants. There wasn't much we could do except groan and laugh in that bemused parent way. I dug a cloth out of the diaper bag; Aaron stuffed it down his pants to try to absorb some of the milk; the guy sitting next to him sighed and shifted slightly away in his seat.

At our layover we headed straight to the airport bathroom, me pushing Sylvia's stroller, Aaron walking gingerly with his wet crotch. To our joy we found a "family bathroom" (yay!)—a single room rather than multiple stalls, a godsend when you have luggage and a stroller and a diaper bag. Or when you need a private place to change your pants, which are soaked through with baby puke.

Aaron opened the door to enter. Just then, a passing woman shot him a dirty look. "That's a *family* bathroom," she spat, shook her head, and walked on grimly. She hadn't noticed us, his family, standing just behind him.

Aaron laughed, but I felt indignant on his behalf. He had *earned* that trip to the family bathroom. Because that damp life lesson, in its own small way, was part of what our ancient rabbis call *tza'ar gidul banim*—the "pain of raising children."

Tza'ar gidul banim. I'm grateful to the rabbis for this phrase. Do we have an equivalent in English? I don't think so. Yes, there's a lot of conspiratorial eye-rolling about sleepless nights, and toddler tantrums, and (in the teen years ahead) "bigger kids, bigger problems," as the expression goes. But I don't know of an English phrase that so neatly and matter-of-factly encapsulates the pain of being a parent.

A lapful of milk is, of course, a minuscule experience of this pain. It's temporary, and with the added distance of time and dry pants, hilarious. But it is, I think, still a good example of tza'ar gidul banim.

The pain comes in all sizes—tiny, small, large, vast. It is sometimes temporary, sometimes permanent, sometimes in-between. It's accompanied by tremendous joy, which is easier to talk about. But it is also important to acknowledge the rainbow of heartbreak that accompanies any human love. Especially the love of something as uncontrollable as another human, who is just beginning her journey through life.

Tza'ar gidul banim: this single phrase describes an impossibly broad range of parental experience. It's the psychedelic intensity of staring into a newborn's eyes; the twinge of a three-year-old screaming "I hate you!" when you make them leave the park after a mind-numbing hour of swing pushing; whatever unimaginable difficulties lie ahead in the teenage years and beyond. And sometimes it's just the physical discomfort of sitting with milk-wet pants for three hours on an airplane.

We are lucky to be parents. Raising children is not only a commandment—"Be fruitful and multiply"— but also a blessing. Jewish tradition is clear on that; when God assures Abraham that his descendants will be as numerous at the stars in the sky, that's a good thing!

But not all blessings are easy. And being honest about that fact—at the very least, with ourselves—is liberating. Instead of pretending that parenting is one constant state of bliss, it helps to acknowledge, as the rabbis do, that sometimes this blessing can be painful. It's okay if we need to pause and give ourselves the emotional equivalent of a family bathroom: some small pleasure, a little extra space, even if it's just a moment of self-acknowledgment that this is hard work that we're doing.

And then we can come back to the sweet moments. To the pure delight in my daughter's face as she retells the story now, at the wise old age of five. I smile, watching as she explodes into laughter at the thought of her baby-self puking in her beloved dad's lap.

To her, it's just a silly story. But I hope on some level she understands the story's deeper meaning: that we're here for her, no matter what—even when things get hard, no matter how much it hurts. Underneath that pain, that tza'ar gidul banim, is love. An infinite, almost superhuman love that can hold anything she throws at us.

Even if it's bound to hurt sometimes.

2

To a Friend Who Named Her Baby Today

We give birth to miracles. And part of the miracle is that we give life away; we create it, we embody it, and we let it go.

Dear N.,

Because (like me) you are Jewish, you gave your baby her name in a special ceremony, surrounded by family, who were laughing and also crying.

Because (like mine) your ancestors are from Poland and Russia, we celebrated with bagels and whitefish and herring and vodka.

Because (like me) you live in Portland, Oregon, we also celebrated with artisanal donuts.

We gathered in a small yoga studio, shoeless, joyful, forming a circle around you and the baby. You poured a bit of warm water on her tiny feet in a sign of respect and welcome. You blessed her with a long and beautiful life. You and your partner announced the baby's name, which no one knew before that moment, not even your mother.

And you cried, a lot, as you read your blessings out loud to your newborn. You kept saying, "This is not going well," even though we all knew it was proceeding perfectly, that your love for her was so profound—and the transition to motherhood so powerful—that your tears were the kind that meant everything is as it should be.

You recalled those she was named after, those who had come before her, her great-grandparents who lived in Poland when World War II began—the ones who escaped, the ones who didn't.

You said you had hoped to bring this baby into a world that was safe and just for all people. You acknowledged that this is not the case. Not yet.

You made it through the speech.

We recited the ancient priestly blessing over your baby as she slept, wrapped in her father's prayer shawl, which was about twenty times bigger than her body. She looked cozy and happy.

I was in your situation not so long ago: my hormones a Jackson Pollock in progress, my body a basketball deflated only slightly by giving birth, my sense of who I was shattered and blossoming wildly all at once.

Dear N., I know that part of why you cried so hard is that it's impossibly scary, bringing a helpless baby into this world. We have seen it with our own eyes: public figures preach hatred, and tens of thousands hang on their every word.

But thousands of years of Jewish experience also teach us that this is nothing new—and there will always be people who resist.

We grew up hearing the stories. We know that hatred and evil will recur, as they always have, and it will be our job—and the job of our children, when they are old enough—to fight those dark forces.

Every year on Purim, we read a story in which an evil advisor directs a foolish king toward genocide; every year on Passover, we read a story in which a tyrant refuses to let our people go. But on both of those holidays, we also celebrate, because we are still here. Still here to tell the stories of these long-ago empires. Still here to teach those stories to our children, to bring as much light as we can into the world during the short time that we're here.

The beginning of Ecclesiastes is often translated "Vanity of vanities, all is vanity."

To be clear: The seventeenth-century translators meant *vanity* as "emptiness," not "self-obsession" in the modern sense. But even that doesn't quite capture the fact that in Hebrew the line also means something more like "Breath, breath, all is breath."

Ecclesiastes is telling us that the whole world is as impermanent and intangible as the steam that comes out of our mouths as we exhale. It's gone before we know it, a miracle that we are here at all.

Our bodies are miracles. We give birth to miracles. And part of the miracle is that we give life away; we create it, we embody it, and we let it go.

So, N., we do what we can while we are here. We love our children fiercely. We teach them to fight for justice, to learn the traditions, to serve others, to love themselves, to love beyond themselves. One day it will be their job to teach their children the same thing. And so it goes.

The baby namings, and the songs, and the holidays, and the carbohydrates: these things bring us together. We keep our tradition strong, and in exchange, it keeps us strong. Through the darkest times, and also the most joyful times. We'll get through this together. Mazel tov.

With love,
Alicia

3
Goodbye, Comfort Zone

I used to think that brokenness was the opposite of the divine spark. But in the mystical Jewish creation myth, you can't have one without the other.

When I was eight months pregnant, I met my friend Annette for coffee. She had a two-year-old, and I was hoping to get a sense of what might lie ahead. She slid gracefully into her chair as I wobbled onto mine. I'd worn my fanciest wrap dress, its sash tied just above my globe-shaped belly, making it protrude even more.

"Aw," she said, eyeing me. "I remember that stage. Your belly looks so cute from the outside, but I remember how it felt from the inside. It was really intense."

She was right; that solid-looking roundness that preceded me everywhere felt less "cute" and more like what it was, a complicated amalgamation of tiny elbows and feet that kicked me when I least expected it. The one thing that actually felt cute was the hiccups that occasionally began ticking like a watch below my belly button.

I think what Annette meant was this: growing a life inside you looks simple from the outside, but it's actually pretty intense. The bigger my belly grew, the more I thought about this quote from the Talmud: "Whoever saves a person's life, it is as if they have saved the whole world."

If saving a human is the equivalent of saving a world, does that mean *creating* a human is the equivalent of creating a world? Did that make me and my fellow moms-to-be a little bit like God?

And what, exactly, might it have felt like for God?

The familiar creation story in Genesis is linear—a day for land and water, then one for the sun and moon; another for fish and birds, then another for animals and humans. This story appears simple and self-explanatory, much as my belly appeared to be a smooth, self-contained globe.

But Jewish mystical texts offer a very different lens on God's creation of the world. According to this account, at first, God was everywhere: an infinite light without any boundary or edge. In order to create the world, God had to withdraw, first creating nothingness. Then, in that empty space, God made a world out of perfect clay vessels: beautiful but inanimate.

The final step was creating life. God channeled divine energy into the vessels, and it worked: they began to vibrate.

But then something surprising happened. The vessels couldn't handle the power of the light. They shattered and fell—and on the way down, a spark of divine light embedded itself in each shard. And that is how the world was created.

In this mystical vision, everything in this world—our bodies, the nature that surrounds us, the objects we create—represents the shattered pieces of that original, perfect Creation. Everything is broken, but also sacred.

Instead of the familiar step-by-step assembly of the world, in which each stage unfolds with the precision of an assembled bunk bed, the mystical retelling is a narrative of experiments and mistakes. Of breaking and falling, and also of landing exactly where we need to be.

To me as a mother, this mystical version of Creation taps into a deep truth: in order to create, we first have to break something.

To make a quilt, you have to cut up material; then you can sew it back together beautifully. To make challah, you have to smash the eggs against the counter and plunge your clean hands into the sticky dough; only then can your bread rise in the oven as a single golden braid.

I used to think that brokenness was the opposite of the divine spark. But in the mystical creation myth, you can't have one without the other. To exist as a human in this world is to experience that unique, bittersweet combination of jagged edges and Godly light.

And to become a parent is to hold these truths together: the miracle and the brokenness, the beauty and the mess.

4

The Miracle of Life Begins with Housework

There's is a fine line between the ordinary work of daily existence and the hugely transformative moments that change our lives forever.

Like any pregnant woman with a hippie streak, I spent months and months reading birth stories. A lot of birth stories. Like, probably way too many. There I was, feet propped on a table, a book propped on my giant belly, seeking inspiration from the many who had preceded me on this path.

Somewhere around the hundredth birth story, I noticed a surprising theme: very often, the miracle of life begins with housework.

In so many birth stories, the mother goes into labor and immediately . . . picks up a broom. She tidies the house, makes breakfast for her other kids, gets them to school, cooks food for later on, and tackles one last organizing project. Only once the contractions get more intense does she retreat into her own world.

Why did this make such an impression on me? I always imagined giving birth as such a big deal that the moment labor began, everything else would just fall away. And that often does happen, later in the process. But early on, these mothers stay in their ordinary lives, taking care of business as long as they can, even while they're on the threshold of this utterly transformative experience.

I wondered at first if this stemmed from a general lack of support for moms. After all, if you know you're going to have to deal with the mess yourself, it's easier to do it before the baby's born. But when my own early labor kicked in, I realized these women weren't cooking and cleaning simply out of a sense of duty. In those intense, anticipatory moments of early labor, I myself felt a strong need to be up, moving around, doing something to keep me busy and focused as I waited for the contractions to strengthen. The housework itself felt like an external manifestation of some sort of inner preparation for birth.

There is, in fact, a fine line between the ordinary work of daily existence—scrubbing pots, mopping floors, folding laundry, answering emails—and the hugely transformative moments that change our lives forever. Housekeeping and the sublime are sometimes impossible to separate.

This is true in day-to-day life and also in Torah. Take, for example, the final chapters of the book of Numbers. There's a recap of the Israelites' desert wanderings, and details about inheritance rights, and the legal difference between murder and manslaughter. Nothing too dramatic. But in between those sections, bam! Without fanfare, we get the story of the death of their great leader, Aaron, who was Moses's brother and the first high priest: "Aaron the priest ascended Mount Hor at God's command and died there, in the fortieth year after the Israelites had left the land of Egypt, on the first day of the fifth month. Aaron was a hundred and twenty-three years old when he died on Mount Hor" (Numbers 33:38–39).

It feels a bit jarring that the Torah describes Aaron's death so casually, in just a couple of sentences—especially when we've just spent so much time on a detailed travelogue of the Israelites' wanderings. Perhaps that's why Rashi, one of the most important medieval Torah commentators, takes a moment to explore this account of Aaron's death.

Rashi focuses on the beginning of this passage: "Aaron the priest ascended Mount Hor at God's command." He points out that the Hebrew words usually translated "at God's command" literally mean "by the mouth of God." When the Torah tells us that Aaron ascended by the mouth of God, Rashi proposes, it's actually saying that he experienced the rare, mystical concept of "the kiss of God": a peaceful, painless death, experienced only by the holiest humans.

I was moved by how similar this Torah passage is to those birth stories in the books I propped on my massive belly. A great passage is coming, but first, there is business to be settled. The details need to be arranged, wanderings written down so they wouldn't be lost, laws notated, precedents set. Like the mothers in early labor, Aaron takes care of the Israelites right up until the moment of transition. Only then is he ready to climb up the mountain alone and bravely face the unknown future.

I was moved, too, by this conception of the Divine. In Jewish tradition, God has many metaphorical faces; this story paints God as a benevolent force, kissing us out of this world when it's our time to go. Perhaps this form of the Divine is one we can connect to during birthing-times. If death can be eased by the kiss of God, why not birth? Why not other major transitions too?

God as a compassionate guide across the border between life and death. God as healer, midwife, lover. God who keeps us silent company while we clean the house and, when we are ready, kisses us into the next part of our story.

5
Let There Be Mama

In Jewish tradition, words are not just random combinations of sounds; they are connected with the essence of things themselves.

I thought briefly about changing my name when I got married. The idea of sharing a last name sounded romantic, and Aaron and I talked about making up a new one that combined ours. But as our wedding date approached, we both had to admit that we each liked our own name. Plus, we were too lazy to think about getting new passports, driver's licenses, and credit cards . . . ugh.

So for three and a half decades, I lived with the same name. Then I had a baby. And just like that, I had a brand-new name: Mama.

Names are a big deal in Jewish tradition. Take, for example, the famous story from Genesis of Jacob wrestling with an angel. After a long night of struggle, the angel finally asks Jacob to let him go. Jacob responds, "I will not let you go until you bless me."

And so the angel blesses him, not with riches or descendants, but with a new name: Israel, "one who struggles with God." It's a complicated name, reflecting both Jacob's specific situation—an all-night wrestling match with an angel—*and* the ongoing Jewish tradition of relating to the Divine with a certain chutzpah.

Jacob isn't the first biblical character to have a surprise name change. His grandfather, Abraham, was raised as Abram (in Hebrew, Avram)—until one day God showed up and declared that he'd be the father of a new people and would go by a new name. From then on, Abram was Abraham.

The Jewish practice of intentional name changing continues to this day. The most common example is when a very ill person changes their name as a step toward healing; others give themselves a Hebrew name upon conversion or when they deepen an existing relationship with Judaism.

This practice reflects the idea that names are connected, on a profound level, to our souls and destinies. And this makes sense, because in Jewish tradition, words are not just random combinations of sounds; they are connected with the essence of things themselves. This is neatly expressed, in Hebrew, by the word *davar*, which means both "word" and "thing." A word, on some level, *is* the thing it represents. That's why, in Genesis, God creates simply by speaking the names of things. "Let there be light," God says, and just like that, light exists.

Names matter.

Like Abraham, like Jacob, I have a new name now. And I'm not the only one: my punk rock, bassist husband, Aaron, is now Papa (or Dad, depending on the day). And since I'm the first of my sisters to have a kid, my tiny newborn has magically transformed a whole group of people into aunts and uncles, grandmas and grandpas.

New names are precious. As our rabbis say, "The earned name is worth much more than the given name" (Ecclesiastes Rabbah 7:4). It's not always easy to transition to a new name; sometimes we have to earn it, as Jacob had to wrestle for his. And just as Jacob never stopped wrestling with God, sometimes the struggle continues long after the name has been earned.

To change our name is to change our fate, to begin a dramatically new chapter of our lives. For me, this new chapter is my life as a mother. Like an angel, my daughter came down into my life, gave me a new name, and changed my destiny.

She named me Mama.

6
Real Life Is All We Have

There's a simple reason to be careful about making vows:
they can make our lives harder than they need to be.

W hen I was pregnant with Sylvia, I went to a fancyish garden party. There was a mom there I watched closely—a beautiful brunette in a yellow sundress, with an adorable little baby she wore strapped to her chest in a purple carrier. I watched in awe as the mom gracefully unclipped the shoulder straps of her carrier in one fluid move and handed her baby to her partner. Then I watched in horror as she walked away to get a drink with the carrier still clipped to her waist, hanging down like some weird lower-front backpack. She left it there for the whole party.

At that moment, I silently whispered a vow to myself: "When I have my baby, and I go to a nice party," I thought, "I'll *never* walk around with a carrier strapped to my waist. I'll take off the damn thing and stick it under a bench!"

You can probably guess what happened after I had my baby. On the extremely rare occasions I made it to anything resembling a garden party, did I take the empty carrier off my waist? No. In fact, I absolutely positively could not have cared less what anyone thought about the baby carrier hanging off my waist. And once in a while I retroactively gave my past self dirty looks for thinking she knew anything about anything.

This is just one example of the countless times I've found myself doing things I'd sworn I would never do.

I deeply regret to say that I was very certain about so much before I became a mom. About what kind of pregnant lady I'd be (cute, active, surprisingly fit); what kind of birth I'd have ("natural," empowering); and what kind of mom I would be (cute, active, not too emotional).

These projections went out the window during week eight of my pregnancy, when I realized that eating an entire bag of gingersnaps would cure my morning sickness.

Cute pregnant lady? Not so much. Given the choice between eating those gingersnaps and barfing my way through work, I devoured the gingersnaps. A whole bag, every day. And from there it continued. One by one, I let go of almost all my vows about what I'd be like—first as a pregnant lady, then as a mom.

Life is unpredictable; we aren't in control; everything changes. I thought I knew these things, but it turned out I didn't really *know* them. For me, it took having kids to learn those lessons, to fully understand that my expectations had very little to do with reality.

Maybe that's why Jewish tradition is so freaked out about the power of making vows—because a vow is all about expectations for the future.

The Torah takes the act of vowing very seriously: "If a man makes a vow to Adonai or takes an oath imposing an obligation on himself, he shall not break his pledge. He must carry out all that has crossed his lips" (Numbers 30:3).

In other words, I should have thought twice before saying to myself, "I'll *never* do *that* when I'm a mom."

There is a time and place for vows. We promise to walk beside our partners into an uncertain future; to love and support our children; to honor our parents and friends. These are deep, serious vows about deep, serious stuff. And that's what makes them worth taking.

But all the other promises we make to ourselves about how the future will be? Not so important. How we'll feel and act when we're pregnant. How fast we'll get back in shape. Whether we'll let our kids cry it out or not. Whether we'll work outside the home or not. Exactly how many grams of sugar or minutes of screen time they'll get. How clean we'll keep the house. Whether or not we'll leave baby carriers strapped around our waists at parties.

I thought I knew the answers to these questions and a million others. But I was wrong.

When the Torah warns us to be careful about taking vows, it uses the language of rules and commandments. But even for the rule-and-commandment averse among us, there's a simple reason to be careful about making vows: they can make our lives harder than they need to be.

The more flexibility we can give ourselves—the fewer vows we make—the easier it is to deal with reality. In the absence of vows, we are free to look at what actually is, instead of the way we thought it would be. And this flexibility allows us to adjust more gracefully to the fact that everything changes: our kids, our friendships, our partners, our bodies, ourselves.

It's possible to be too flexible, of course. Some vows and intentions are central, non-negotiable, and fundamental: our standards for how we're treated by our partners, for example, or caring for our own health, or making sure our kids are safe. So, when we begin to notice something we swore we'd never allow to happen, it's worth asking: is this one of my core values or just an expectation I had before I knew what parenthood would really be like?

Should I hold on to this vow, or let it go?

For our essential truths, we do what we can to honor them, even when it's difficult. For everything else, the silly little ways we thought we'd be—well, bring on the gingersnaps, the screen time, the unwashed hair, the overpriced Play-Doh, the dangling baby carrier, the messy kitchen, and all the other imperfect detritus of our lives.

The mom-life that doesn't look quite how we thought it would? That's real life, and it's all we have.

7

Things We Used to Know

We are instinctively gentle with newborn babies.
It can be harder to be gentle with ourselves in our own
transition as new mothers.

When Aaron and I decided we were ready to start a family, I was excited but not nervous. After all, I'd taught elementary school before and already knew what sort of parent I wanted to be: compassionate but firm; fun, but also in charge. My experience teaching other people's kids had trained me to balance clear expectations with an openness to the small human in front of me. And as a bonus, I had my own excellent mother as an example. "You'll be a natural," people said to me—and though I would politely demur, I secretly believed they were right.

But when I became a mom, I didn't *feel* like a natural. I felt like a purse someone had turned upside down and dumped out on the floor. For nine months I'd walked around with this beautiful treasure in me; now I was just sort of . . . empty.

"You'll come back to yourself," an older friend said to me when Sylvia was just a few weeks old. Until she said that, I'd been trying my best to pretend everything was fine. Was it so obvious that I was lost? And (now that she mentioned it) was there even a *self* to come back to?

It turned out my friend was right. As time went on, I did grow into the kind of mother I'd wanted to be. I don't really believe in the word *natural* anymore, but at least I came to have some idea of what I was doing; the experience of motherhood changed into something resembling what I'd expected, and I began to recognize myself again.

The mysterious transition to motherhood involves so much letting go. A lifetime of carefully accumulated skills suddenly turns (temporarily) irrelevant. Honed the ability to negotiate contracts, speak another language, or remember a whole table's orders without writing them down? Great. But that's not going to help you get through the next few months.

According to Jewish tradition, it's not only the mother who must lose something during the transition into her new life. The baby, too, has to let go of what it knows in order to be born.

This process is described in one of my favorite legends from the Talmud. It begins with a vision of an angel visiting a fetus inside the mother's womb. First, the angel teaches the baby-to-be the entire Torah: all the sacred traditions and laws and stories, luminously transmitted into this pure being. Then, just before birth, the angel strikes the baby's mouth, and she forgets what she has learned. Only then is she ready to be born.

I love this story, because while our instinct is often to hold on tightly to all we've gained, this legend is about the power of letting go. Learning the whole Torah is just the beginning; to be born, we have to forget it.

This resonates with another biblical imagination of pregnancy. In Psalm 139, a love poem to God, the poet envisions a developing human embryo: "For You formed my inward parts; You knitted me together in my mother's womb. . . . Your eyes saw my unformed substance; in Your book were written . . . the days that were formed for me, before they existed."

Before we're born, we are all possibility and potential: "unformed substance." But birth doesn't end the fact that we live in mystery, and we never know quite what's coming next. This fact is more obvious at certain inflection points: birth, adolescence, leaving home, waiting for medical test results, new parenthood. But the truth is that as long as we are alive, each one of us is in process, our unwritten days slowly being written as we live them. And comfortingly, in this poetic description, though we are suffused in mystery, we are also profoundly known by God—just as my wise friend knew things about my experience I couldn't yet see.

We are instinctively gentle with newborn babies. It's so easy to see how much they depend on us, how helpless they are in the face of all they do not know. It can be harder to be gentle with ourselves in our own transition as new mothers. To recognize that we are not supposed to land in a new stage of life perfectly prepared; that's not how it works.

Sometimes, in order to be born, in order to grow, we have to forget the Torah we knew so well. Only then can we begin to learn it again.

And when it's time, we come back to ourselves. Deeper, wiser, with more of our story written but still surrounded by mystery.

8
Was God in Labor?

Rereading the creation story as a mother, I wonder:
did God have to give something up to create the world too?

We often think of creation as making something out of
nothing (fancy Latin: *ex nihilo*). And this model jibes with
the biblical creation story—from a massive nothingness, God
begins to create the world piece by piece. Language is the only
tool God uses here, creating with simple, direct phrases: "Let
there be light," "Let there be land," "Let there be humans."

We often think of creativity this way too. An artist begins
with a blank expanse, covers it in colors, and voilà: a painting.
A builder takes an empty plot of land, builds on it, and there's a
house. A baby is born, and magically, a tiny human exists where
before there was just air.

But was there really *nothing* there before the new creation?
Did they really start from scratch?

As the mother of a tiny human, I have this nagging sense that
something was there before my baby . . . I can almost remember . . .

Oh yeah, that was what I called "my life." And it wasn't just a
blank space. I actually really liked it!

I enjoyed long, unbroken work sessions, evening drinks with
friends, weekend brunches in crowded restaurants, quiet walks
around the block. And other, smaller pleasures too, ones I didn't
even appreciate yet—like traveling without checking three bags
plus a stroller plus a car seat, then lugging a carry-on stuffed with
disposable diapers and chewy toys through the airport.

Don't get me wrong. Sylvia is a miracle, an absolute joy, the
single best thing that ever happened to me. When she toddles

over to hug me, my heart breaks open like a rainbow geode. I've been known to stay up late looking at pictures of her after she goes to sleep.

And yet, it's simply a truth: my old life is over.

Rereading the creation story now as a mother, I wonder: did God have to give something up to create the world too?

According to medieval Jewish mystics, the answer is yes. In the very beginning, they explain, God was everywhere—an infinite light that filled the universe from one end to the other. There was no space for heaven, earth, oceans, humans, clouds, or chocolate.

In order to create space for this universe, God had to withdraw. In Hebrew this withdrawal is called *tzimtzum*. Sometimes the word is even translated as "contraction," which I love, because . . . how great is it to imagine God in labor?

Tzimtzum. God couldn't take up all that space and create a world too. So God pulled that luminous God-self back, making a sort of black hole at the center of the universe.

Only then, in that void, was there room. Room for the planets and the sky and the jungles and the dinosaurs and the stars and the trees and, eventually, people. Our oldest ancestors, all the way down to you and me. And our little human babies.

Struggling through the transition into my new life as a mother, the idea of tzimtzum helped me. It was easy to blame myself, to think I was selfish for struggling to let go of my previous life. But the more I thought about tzimtzum, the more I realized that it wasn't just a personal failing.

After all, the kabbalists understood this basic spiritual truth back in the Middle Ages. To create something, you also have to withdraw a little bit. To make a new life, you have to give up something of your old life. It hurts sometimes; that's okay. It's worth it.

9
Motherhood Brings Out My Superstitious Side

We want to hold on to what we have. But there's no better illustration of impermanence than our quickly changing little ones. And so we must also practice letting go.

D uring the first few weeks of my son Elijah's life, I was overwhelmed by gratitude. Every hour or so I found myself newly bowled over by the beauty, mystery, and ridiculous cuteness of this little guy in a frog onesie.

It was almost too much. What could I do with all that raw emotion, that overwhelming love? How could I express my gratitude for such an intense blessing? What does Jewish tradition say about this beautiful feeling of overwhelming appreciation?

One traditional Jewish approach to massive joy—counterintuitively, for a culture that often expresses emotions enthusiastically—is to keep our mouths shut.

This approach derives from the ancient superstition that if you name the good things in your life, evil spirits might get jealous and come take your blessings away. (Not necessarily the most psychologically healthy approach, but there you have it.)

Whisper your gratitude to God, sure; stare at your beautiful kiddo for hours on end; but whatever you do, don't talk about how gorgeous he is.

The idea is that we can avoid attracting evil spirits by not mentioning the good stuff. And if we *must* speak about our blessings, we also can drive those bad vibes away by making a spitting noise directly afterward. "Yes, we're all healthy, *tfutfutfu*," a person might say, or "She's beautiful, *pupupu*."

Weird as this spitting custom is, I secretly find it sort of reassuring. We love so deeply, and we control so little. It's only natural to try to hold on tightly to beauty and joy, and avoid risking it at all costs. But the Torah also offers another, very different approach to receiving blessings.

In the book of Deuteronomy, we are instructed that when we receive a blessing, the first thing we should do is to let it go. Or at least, let *part* of it go.

Specifically, God tells the Israelites that after they enter the Holy Land and begin to farm, they must gather the first of their produce in a basket and bring it to the Temple. There, they will present it as an offering: bowing low in humility, expressing gratitude, and giving this first taste of God's bounty back to God.

These two Jewish traditions of how to receive blessing are almost diametrically opposed. In one, we clutch the blessing tightly—in the other, we let it go. Being a parent, we experience both of these every day.

We want to hold on to what we have: our precious babies, our moments of sweet equilibrium. But there's no better illustration of impermanence than our quickly changing little ones. And so we must also practice letting go, at least a little bit, every single day.

I think we're fortunate to have these two approaches in our tradition. I may not "believe" in superstition, but am I going to stop saying a quiet *pupupu* when I mention my blessings? Uh, no. I deal with anxiety in my daily life, and it's a pretty simple way to make me feel better.

At the same time, deep down, I know that the second approach—letting go, at least a little—is profoundly important too. It may not be my natural response, but it's one worth cultivating: To loosen my grip. To let these beautiful moments happen without clinging to them.

To bow low, to give back; even as I give thanks, to let go.

10

To a Mama Friend Who Is Having a Hard Time

I was feeling the curve of the Möbius strip, where welcoming new life means a small kind of death.

Dear Mama,

I've never been a fan of the "God only gives us what we can handle" theory. Is that supposed to mean extra-rough things happen only to people who are better equipped to deal with them? No way—I just don't believe that.

But, paradoxically, I do believe the opposite of that line. We become stronger through dealing with difficulty. And that is exactly what you are doing.

I saw how excited you were to become a mom, I see how much you love your baby, and I see how incredibly hard things are for you right now. And as someone who has been there, I am writing to say that I see you, and I'm sorry, and I love you.

One thing I love about the Torah is how it does not shy away from acknowledging the difficulty of life. Our holy traditions are pretty clear-eyed about how hard it is to be human. And I think that's why, toward the very end of the Torah, when Moses is preparing to die, he goes very deep in his parting speech.

Moses's dramatic declaration to the assembled Israelites ends with these words: "I have put before you life and death, blessing and curse. Choose life" (Deuteronomy 30:19).

When I was younger, and saw things in black and white, I used to think this passage was saying that there are two separate paths—one of life and blessing, one of death and curse—and we should choose the first.

But now I think it's more complicated. Life and death, blessing and curse—these words are pairs of opposites, but they're also impossible to untangle from one another.

After all, doesn't every new life create a death? In the natural cycle, doesn't the death of any living thing give way to new life?

And though I'm not exactly sure what *curse* even means, I do know that every shitty situation contains some hidden blessings—just as every blessing contains some unforeseen challenges.

As a mother, I now read Moses's admonition not as a binary, but as a paradox. Life and death, blessing and curse are one single, paradoxical, interwoven path—a Möbius strip, like marriage or motherhood.

As Rebecca Solnit writes in *A Field Guide to Getting Lost*, "Sometimes gaining and losing are more intimately related than we like to think."

Moses's own mother would have understood this. When he was a baby, she placed him in a basket and sent him floating away to save his life. She said goodbye to him forever in order to make sure he would survive, like those haunting stories of Jewish parents in Holocaust-era Europe who sent their children away on the Kindertransport trains.

At 120 years old and about to die himself, Moses understands how impossible it is to disentangle life and death, blessing and curse. He has seen firsthand how liberation came through plagues, how freedom led to thirst. He has witnessed God's magnificent presence, received the beautiful Torah of black fire on white fire—but he has also watched God's light burn so brightly it killed his nephews.

Still, at the end of his own life, this is the advice Moses gives us, while we are still in the middle of ours: choose life.

Dear Mama, our stories are different, but I, too, have cried myself to sleep every night beside my baby. I was feeling the curve of the Möbius strip, where welcoming new life means a small kind of death. Each of us has our own story. In mine, we could no longer afford to live in the city I loved, and we moved far away from my family and friends. I had to start over, to make a new life as a mother. It was a difficult beginning.

Blessing and challenge all rolled up in one complicated, confusing, glorious, demanding, unpredictable path. This pain reminds me of another quote from Rebecca Solnit, in which she describes "the anguish of the butterfly, whose body must disintegrate and reform more than once in its life cycle."

My dear butterfly mama, I wish I could make it easier for you. I wish we didn't have to disintegrate to be reborn. But I also know that, as they say in Hebrew, *Gam zeh ya'avor*—"This too shall pass." The good times don't last forever, but neither do the hard parts; it's all rolled up together, and none of it lasts.

And as long as we are here, this is what we do: we choose life.

11

The Definition of Sacrifice Sounds a Lot Like Parenthood

Every offering was an opportunity to connect with the Divine.

During the first decade or so of my dating life, whenever I got in a fight with a partner, I believed I should sacrifice my own perspective in order to see theirs. I thought the high road was to transcend my own limited point of view, to resist my natural desire to advocate for my needs, and to meet their needs instead.

But one day in my early twenties, I suddenly remembered Hillel's famous saying, found in *Pirkei Avot* (*Ethics of the Fathers*): "If I am not for myself, who will be for me?" (*Pirkei Avot* 1:15).

From that moment on, I decided I was done. No more sacrificing my own needs for another's; I was going to be my own advocate from now on.

That served me extremely well for a number of years. Then I became a mom. And as I quickly found out, parenting a newborn definitely called for my old relationship paradigm of pushing past my own needs and putting my daughter first.

Take, for example, the first week after my C-section. After major surgery at any other time in my life, I would have focused on resting, healing, and getting enough sleep so my body could repair itself. If anyone had tried waking me up every two hours all night long to suck on my boob, I would have banished them from my life immediately. "Can't you see I just got sliced in half?" I would have yelled.

But as a new mom, it was utterly clear—overlooking my own needs was part of the deal. Yes, I needed to heal, but even more, my helpless newborn needed love, attention, and, yes, to suck on my boob every two hours. And as hard as it was to drag myself awake, I was happy to do it.

After the intensity of the newborn months, the need to push past my own desires grew less physically demanding . . . but it's still a big part of parenting. I want to sit on the couch and read? Too bad; naptime's over, we have to go to the park. I want to talk to my friend on the phone? Too bad; I have to keep Sylvia from eating the sand in the sandbox. Overlooking my own desires for the sake of something bigger is now pretty much the way I spend my time.

I'm uncomfortable using the word *sacrifice* to describe these basic, constant acts of caring for my daughter. After all, I *chose* this path. I asked to bring a child into the world, and I was lucky enough to receive this incredible little peanut. And as I'm sure she'll point out in her tween years, she never asked to be born.

And yet I do have to admit that *Webster's* definition of *sacrifice* as "giving up something you want to do . . . especially in order to help someone" is a decent description of my daily parenting reality.

So I decided to dig back into the original Jewish idea of sacrifice —from the book of Leviticus and its many chapters about offerings brought by ordinary Israelites and offered by priests on a sacred fire in the ancient Mishkan (Tabernacle), then the Temple. There are animals, grain, incense, and bread; offerings of gratitude, ones to atone for sins, and regular old daily offerings as a way of saying hello to God.

These sacrifices ended when the Temple was destroyed, two thousand years ago. But the rules are still there, page after page. And they're famously challenging for modern readers—ritualized, bloody, and intense. Not exactly kid-friendly material.

So it's surprising that in some old-school Jewish circles, small children begin their Torah study with this book. Why would teachers start here, with a list of obscure sacrifices, rather than at the beginning, with the creation of the world?

Some commentators have observed that while the English word *sacrifice* is related to the word *sacred*, the Hebrew word is *korban*, which derives from a root meaning "closeness." So a more literal translation for the Hebrew would be something like "drawing close."

In this interpretation, sacrifices played an important role in the life of the community and the individual: they brought us closer to God. Every offering was an opportunity to connect with the Divine. Perhaps that's one reason for the tradition of beginning children's Torah study here. Children's natural element is closeness and immediacy, which is why they're constantly calling to us, with needs that must be taken care of here and now.

Understood this way, the idea of making sacrifices as a parent takes on a deeper, richer meaning too. Sacrifice transforms from the lament of a frustrated parent into a sacred form of service, a way of drawing closer to our kids (and maybe even to the Divine) by demonstrating our love.

Does this mean we should abandon our dreams, ignoring our own needs to pursue motherly sainthood? Absolutely not. After all, the Torah commands the ancient Israelites to sacrifice animals, grains, and oil—not themselves.

Still, what if we could reframe the practice of relinquishing our desires—letting go of control over our space, our time, and the desire for a floor free of pasta sauce—as sacrifices in the Hebrew sense? A sacred mechanism for drawing close to our children.

The ancient rabbis, too, wondered why children might begin their Torah study with the passage about sacrifices. They came up with a different answer, sweet and rather mysterious. "Since the sacrifices are pure, and the children are pure," they say, "let the pure come and study the pure."

Maybe this is what the rabbis meant: children are pure because they live in the present moment. They are always close to their feelings. We adults are different, prone to distance and distraction. But in showing up for our kids, even when it's not easy, we have the privilege of using the ancient spiritual practice of sacrifice in our own lives. We draw closer to them, and we draw them close to us. And perhaps in that closeness, the Divine Presence hovers between us, held here by our love.

12
The Magic of Asking for Help

Asking for help is not selfish. It is not weak. It does not make us less of a leader—or less of a mother.

A sking for help does not come naturally to me. I've always been independent to the point of stubbornness.

That worked for me until I became a mother. Now, ohmygosh, I need help constantly. And little by little, I'm learning how to ask for it.

Case in point: Because my amazing mother stayed home with us when I was growing up, I had simply assumed I would too. I didn't consider the fact that I was passionate about my career, or that Aaron and I were both self-employed, doing a patchwork combination of playing in bands and doing things that paid our rent (teaching, real estate).

"It'll be simple," we figured. "We'll just take turns watching the baby!"

As it turned out, this was not a good plan, since it meant only one of us could work at a time. Resentment between us built as we jockeyed for much-needed hours. One of us would walk to a coffee shop with our laptop, smiling, while the other stewed in the sun at the playground, seething about looming deadlines. Pro tip: this is bad for a marriage.

It took us over a year to admit that our plan wasn't working and finally start figuring out how we could build a healthy family life, rather than a zero-sum fight for scraps of work time. For me, a big part of this was coming to understand that there was nothing wrong with sending Sylvia to daycare. It wasn't how I grew up, but that didn't mean it was a personal failing. Instead, it was a brave step that would (and did) make me a happier person and a better mother—able to work when I was working and be a mom when I was with Sylvia.

There was something else too: I had to learn to ask Aaron for more help. He is, by nature, a supportive and loving person, and he was always present and involved. For a long time I couldn't imagine how I could ever ask him for more. But the truth was, after Sylvia's birth, I found myself desperately needing all kinds of support I hadn't even wanted before.

I wish I could say I was able to gracefully express this newfound need. Instead, a fiery outpouring of biblical proportions erupted from my mouth every other night, and instead of coming closer, our positions hardened. Was this the best way to go about things? No. But we worked through it, with the help of a couples therapist.

As we found our way back to each other, I learned that Aaron needed my help too—and that as a couple, we needed support in ways we hadn't before. Before we became parents, we took care of ourselves, we took care of each other, the math worked out. But add in the shared responsibility of caring for a tiny helpless human, and we had a whole new equation on our hands.

At the time, I felt overwhelmed and alone. But looking back, I take comfort in the fact that learning to reach out for help seems to be a very common part of adulting—even for people who are already, by all accounts, adults. In fact, Moses himself went through something very similar after leading the Israelites out of Egypt.

After the Exodus, Moses becomes the official leader of the Israelites—a new role. At first he manages well enough on his own, but as time goes on, his responsibilities begin to accumulate. Every time people have a dispute they go directly to him, and before long, he's staggering under the weight of the issues people bring him from morning to night.

His father-in-law, Yitro (Jethro), sees this and steps in. "Why do you act alone?" Yitro asks. Moses explains that the people need him to settle their disputes, but Yitro pushes back: "The thing you are doing is not right; you will surely wear yourself out, and these people as well. For the task is too heavy for you; you cannot do it alone" (Exodus 18:14–18).

Yitro has a practical solution for his son-in-law. He instructs Moses to find wise people and assign them to rule over groups of thousands, hundreds, fifties, and tens. In other words, he teaches Moses how to ask for help.

As soon as this judicial system is created, Moses suddenly has time to do other things, like receive the Ten Commandments—which actually occurs right after this lesson in delegation.

Is this timing a coincidence? I don't think so. Moses could never have ascended Mount Sinai if he were still stuck in the desert from morning to night, playing Judge Judy for all his people's disputes. From a time management perspective, it just doesn't work.

And on a deeper level, I have a hunch that Moses needed to learn to admit his limitations and step back from the fantasy of total control. Only then did he have the inner strength to receive the Ten Commandments, those powerful, epic instructions that would reverberate throughout millennia.

As a mom, Yitro's words to Moses feel like they're directed squarely at me too: "The thing you are doing is not right; you will surely wear yourself out, and these people as well. For the task is too heavy for you; you cannot do it alone."

When Moses was appointed leader of the Israelites, he made the mistake of assuming it was his job to handle their problems all by himself. Three thousand years later, my husband and I made the same mistake, assuming that as leaders of our family, we weren't allowed to call for backup. But Yitro teaches us, as he taught Moses, that asking for help is not selfish. It is not weak. It does not make us less of a leader—or less of a mother. Quite the opposite.

Asking for help, we invite the sacred into our lives.

13

The Beautiful and the Gross

One thing the Torah and mothers have in common:
we are not afraid to talk directly about the grosser parts
of physical existence.

B ecoming a mom is an education in two very different aspects
of the human body: the beautiful and the gross.

There's nothing like the sweetness of a naked baby after a
bath, wrapped up in a big towel. Or the joy of watching a little
one learn to walk or jump. (I didn't realize jumping was its own
developmental benchmark until I got to watch my own sweet
butterball lift her little body off the earth with her own power for
the first time, then giggle and do it again.)

At the same time, amidst all that beauty, any mother of a
young child is up close and personal with multiple bodily fluids
every single day. Poop, pee, snot, tears, rinse, repeat. And that's
on a good day.

It's not just the little bodies either. There's also my own. On
the one hand, what could be more transcendent than serving as a
physical vessel for life, carrying a brand-new human safely through
nine months of growing from a tiny speck to a real live baby?

On the other hand, the reality of postpartum life knocked me
off my feet. I'd looked forward to blissful hours in bed nursing
my newborn, surrounded by a soft glow. What I got instead was
a painful and messy C-section recovery, trouble with milk supply,
and the shocking fact that I was now living in a very different
body than the one I'd known most of my life.

I wish I'd been more prepared for the physical transition to motherhood. But that hadn't really been on my radar at all. The postpartum body was completely missing from all the birthing videos I watched, birth classes I dutifully attended, collections of birth stories I devoured. How was I supposed to know what to expect?

Now that I'm a mom, I get it. When my friends are pregnant, I want to support them, not turn into some oracle of doom with warnings of inflatable donuts and bloody gauze. When they wonder about having a baby, they ask the same questions I once did: about contractions and cloth diapers and baby carriers, not pelvic-floor health.

But the sometimes-shocking, day-to-day physicality of parenting makes me appreciate even more how surprisingly matter-of-fact the Torah often is about the sort of gross bodily details we would usually avoid in polite conversation.

In the book of Leviticus, there is an entire Torah portion called *Tazria*, literally, "one who conceives." It begins by talking about a postpartum mother, detailing how many days after giving birth she is considered ritually impure (sometimes translated as "unclean," but actually a more complicated and at least somewhat less offensive concept).

From these tasty details, the Torah moves on to another bodily issue: *tzara'at*, or biblical leprosy. This isn't medical leprosy as we know it today; instead, it's a mysterious spiritual sickness that affects men, women, and even houses and clothes. Though many ancient rabbis interpreted tzara'at as a punishment for spiritual misbehavior—gossip is the classic example—it manifests in a resolutely physical way, with nasty rashes, ingrown hairs, and other weird growths.

And boy does the Torah go into detail. Reading biblical passages about tzara'at, I'm reminded of the kinds of conversations that happen in a room full of new mothers. Strangers or old friends, it doesn't matter . . . among the coos and exclamations about each other's babies' cuteness, you inevitably end up talking about labor, milk supply, breast infections, pain, and blood.

This, it turns out, is something the Torah and mothers have in common: we are not afraid to talk directly about the grosser parts of physical existence.

Of course, the Torah also acknowledges, as mothers do, that bodies are gorgeous and sacred. According to Genesis, we are made in the image of God; our bodies are a reflection of the Divine. But as this section of the Torah reminds us, that beauty is only half the story.

As physical beings, we are always in transition. We are part of an organic, natural cycle. We blossom, we wane; we are born, we give birth, we die; our bodies tear and heal, are pushed and recover, weaken and strengthen.

As a mom, the messy parts of living in a body are impossible for me to ignore. And although I am inspired by the beautiful idea that we are walking, talking avatars for the Divine, I also love that the Torah talks directly about the gross stuff, from postpartum bleeding to weird skin diseases. Life in a body is complicated, and I appreciate that rather than pretending the gross stuff doesn't exist, the Torah gives us a way to integrate it.

Because the beauty comes and goes, and comes back again; this is part of living in a body. And we mothers are learning these lessons every day, right here, between the miracles and the poop.

PART 2

On the Journey

How to Be Real, How to Love

14
What If I'm Pharaoh?

In trying to hold on to our old lives, we miss out on the blessings that transformation can bring.

Every year at Passover, we tell the story of the Ten Plagues. This story, and the roundness of that famous number, have become so familiar that it's easy to assume there were *always* going to be ten plagues before Pharaoh finally gave in.

But according to the story, that's not really the case. After each plague, God gives Pharaoh the opportunity to change his mind and free the Israelites. Each time, Pharaoh begins to relent, but then he (or, weirdly, God) "hardens his heart" and decides that he *does* need those Israelite slaves after all. And so the plagues keep on going—with worse and worse consequences for the Egyptians—all the way up to ten.

Pharaoh's the villain here; I don't think we're supposed to feel sorry for him.

Reading this story as a mom, though, I find it disturbingly easy to see things from Pharaoh's side. He's lived one way for a long time; now he's supposed to suddenly loosen his grip, become gentle, let go of control?

I find myself feeling oddly . . . sympathetic to Pharaoh now, even though he's clearly the bad guy.

Because it turns out, I'm stubborn like Pharaoh.

This realization started to hit me during my pregnancy. Since I was blessed with an easy ride—no bed rest, no gestational diabetes—I was able to go pretty much full speed ahead with my life. As a musician, for me that meant touring, performing, and recording until two weeks before my due date.

A tour of Italy at seven months pregnant with my bass-playing husband? That sounded pretty safe, and delicious, and romantic to boot.

I should have known better. When you're a scrappy indie musician with a minuscule following and no financial backing, touring is generally a lot less romantic than it sounds. I knew this, but somehow it didn't really hit me until I found myself seven months pregnant, huddled on a small cot above a rock club that blasted music until 2:00 a.m., breathing in the secondhand cigarette smoke that wafted through the air vents beside me.

The last stop on that tour was London, where I noticed that the accessible seats on the Tube have icons of people with various conditions to indicate who the seats are intended for. There was an icon of a person in a wheelchair, one of a person with a cane, and one of a pregnant woman. Her belly was about as big as mine. I'd never seen a sign like that in the States, and it came as a revelation.

A fiercely independent person, I had figured I'd apply the same standards to myself during pregnancy as I always had. I'd push myself as hard as ever, I thought, and I was determined not to ask for special treatment. But, sitting on the Tube in absolute exhaustion, I realized I was wrong.

Carrying a baby is a true physical challenge. And as I clutched my rolly bag and stared at that sign of a pregnant stick figure, I realized that I could be as gentle with myself as whoever decided to put up those stickers. Allowing myself some slack as a pregnant woman would be an act not of weakness but of self-compassion. (Later, I'd realize this applied to motherhood too.)

Back to the Torah: by the seventh plague, Pharaoh has experienced rivers of blood and flaming hail. He probably senses that nothing will stop the Israelites from eventually leaving Egypt—but he still can't let them go. He's built a civilization on forced labor, not compassion, and he can't imagine living any other way. Sometimes he gets close, but soon enough, he slips back into his old habits.

I can relate. That moment on the Tube was just the beginning; it took me months of trying, and failing, to admit that I simply couldn't live the way I had before. I love my work; it's an essential part of my life, and I had no intention of stopping. But forging ahead as if nothing had changed? I used to think I could pull it off. Now I think this denial was actually a form of weakness, not strength. It was me hardening my own heart, Pharaoh-style.

I used to think I had to stay the course no matter what. Anything else, I thought, would be failure. Now I'm learning, just as Pharaoh did, that that's not true. In trying to hold on to our old lives, we miss out on the unforeseen blessings that transformation can bring.

Life doesn't ask for our permission to change all around us. It just changes. But how we deal with that change? That's up to us. That permission lies in our own hearts. We can free ourselves; we can let ourselves go.

15
Climbing Out of the Pit

Everyone said the first year was difficult. I figured I just had to grit my teeth and get through it.

One of the worst family stories in Genesis is about Jacob playing favorites between his sons. He gives Joseph a beautiful coat, which makes Joseph's brothers jealous. Then it gets worse: instead of dealing with that jealousy in a constructive way, Joseph's brothers throw him into a pit, deep in the desert, and then sell him to some passing slave traders.

As a person who loves clothes, I used to focus on the many-colored coat that Jacob gives Joseph. Perhaps that was because I couldn't quite deal with the heartbreaking tale of brothers sending a sibling into exile.

But as a mom, I've been feeling more in touch with heart-break. Reading this story now, I focus not on Joseph's fancy coat but on his harrowing experience. And even though my life is tremendously less dramatic, I resonate with his despair.

Here's what the Torah says about Joseph's darkest moment: "When Joseph came up to his brothers . . . they took him and cast him into the pit. The pit was empty; there was no water in it" (Genesis 37:23–24).

That empty pit feels personal. Because for about a year and a half after my daughter was born, I, too, was in a pit.

It took me fourteen months to realize there was a problem. I was on a plane, landing with major turbulence, holding Sylvia on my lap. As we jolted down toward the fast-approaching tarmac, I found myself thinking with a strange sort of excitement, "Maybe the plane will crash, and I won't have to be here anymore! And it's perfect, because I won't be leaving her alone either."

Thankfully, my next thought was: "What was *that*?!"

That night, we stayed at a friend's house in Oakland. After I'd picked yet another fight with my husband Aaron and he'd gone downstairs unhappily to sleep on our host's couch, I found myself alone in the guest bedroom, searching on my computer for "postpartum depression."

In fact, I'd been doing that intermittently for the last year, late at night, almost automatically, without knowing why. Some part of me had known for a long time that something was off, but that moment on the plane was my first conscious moment of realization.

Joseph was down in the pit because his jealous brothers wanted to get rid of him; my descent was no one's fault. As far as I can tell, it was some invisible combination of factors. Birth and postpartum recovery were rough; I never had enough milk; I never had enough sleep; we'd recently moved across the country with a new baby, away from family and friends.

Add the financial, emotional, and marital stresses of reinventing our lives as parents in a new city, trying to make a tenuous living as freelancers without childcare. And maybe some genetic predisposition, given my maternal grandmother's postpartum psychosis.

Phew. Looking back, it sounds strange that it took fourteen months for me to realize something was wrong.

But I assumed what I was experiencing was normal; after all, everyone said the first year was difficult. I figured that I just had to grit my teeth and get through it. Plus, my self-critical tendencies kicked into high gear, finding ways to blame myself: I'd been spoiled by waiting too long to have a kid; I'd made a stupid career decision to be an artist.

Unlike my grandmother, I didn't have a spectacular breakdown. I didn't have trouble eating, or sleeping, or doing my work. I didn't even have trouble bonding with my baby, as so many women with postpartum depression do.

I was simply miserable and angry, almost all the time.

That's why, as I sat on that plane wishing to crash with my daughter in my arms, my next feeling was relief. The moment I realized I wasn't just lazy or spoiled; I needed help. I was at the bottom of an empty pit.

"The pit was empty; there was no water in it." Torah commentators, reading carefully, pick up on a redundancy in this sentence. If a pit is empty, then of course there's no water in it; and since rabbinic tradition holds that the Torah never wastes words, there must be a reason for that second phrase. They therefore interpret that sentence to mean that there was no water in that pit—but there *were* snakes and scorpions.

Now that I'm safely out of my pit, I've been thinking about those snakes and scorpions. It turns out that in Judaism, although snakes have the power to harm, their image also contains the power to heal. Elsewhere in the Torah, during an epidemic of snakebites, God tells Moses to make a bronze serpent and hold it up on a post to heal anyone who had suffered a lethal snakebite, just by looking at it. Precisely by looking at an image of a snake like the one that bit them in the first place, the wounded are made whole again.

I think these snakes can teach us that healing comes not from looking away from our wounds, but from accepting them. From compassionately embracing our own stories and hearing each other's too.

One of the things that helped me most in my healing was reading articles, essays, and memoirs about other mothers' experiences of difficulty and challenge. Reading their stories, I understood that I wasn't alone. I wouldn't be stuck down in the pit forever. I wasn't a bad mother. I wasn't weak. I wasn't too old, or too stubborn, or not maternal enough.

I was just in a pit, and I needed help getting out. And that realization allowed me to ask for help, and with that help, to climb up out of the pit to the life that had been waiting for me all along.

16
How to Be Real, How to Love

No matter how much he loves the Israelites, Moses cannot lead them alone.

As my second child's due date approached, I could feel my firstborn's only-kid status slipping away. This time around, having a baby wouldn't just transform *my* life; it was going to be a big change for Sylvia too.

I was excited for her to have a sibling, I was nervous about balancing two kids, and I was terrified about how my "spirited" two-year-old would deal with the adjustment to having a younger brother.

She'd already done a good job of teaching me that I couldn't control how she'd react. The only thing I could control was how I could guide our family through this transition. And I figured I'd look for inspiration in the ultimate transition shepherd: Moses.

As the book of Deuteronomy begins, Moses, too, is preparing his flock for a major transition. For me, that transition was giving birth; for Moses, his own death. And while my biggest worry was how my toddler would handle the transition, Moses is focused on how to help his people, who have relied on his leadership for an entire generation, prepare to continue without him.

Moses begins by telling the Israelites the history of their wanderings. He gives them short verbal snapshots of all the places they've stopped in the desert, highlights along the way, and key moments in their travels.

At first this seems like the ancient equivalent of the slide-shows people make for *b'nei mitzvah*: a recap of greatest hits, sweet moments across the years. But then I came upon a moment, mixed in among the lists of place names, when Moses takes a break from the details of the Israelites' wanderings and gets surprisingly personal.

Speaking frankly about his mixed feelings as a parent figure to the children of Israel, Moses recalls a moment of doubt he experienced years earlier:

> I said to you, "I cannot bear the burden of you by myself. Adonai your God has multiplied you until you are today as numerous as the stars in the sky. May Adonai, the God of your ancestors, increase your numbers a thousandfold and bless you as God promised you. How can I bear unaided the trouble of you, and the burden, and the bickering! Pick from each of your tribes men who are wise, discerning, and experienced, and I will appoint them as your heads." (Deuteronomy 1:9–13)

I'm so moved by the vulnerability in this speech. Rather than pretending to be the perfect leader, looking back on the past with only positive feelings, Moses speaks to his people with raw, tender, practical honesty. He frankly reveals his own insecurity in a way leaders rarely do in public life, even today.

On one hand, he explains, he loves them, knows their very existence is a miracle from God, and wants only blessings for them. At the same time, with "the burden, and the bickering," they were super hard to deal with in the moment. And even in this big public speech at the end of his life, Moses doesn't gloss over that difficulty.

No matter how much he loves the Israelites, Moses cannot lead them alone. He needs their help; he needs them to look out for each other as well. This is a paradoxical part of being a leader, or a parent: doing our job well is an odd combination of caretaking and teaching others to care for themselves and for each other.

We can be real—even as leaders, even as moms. We can be authentic and vulnerable and still create a space where our children know they are safe. We can hold our little tribe together and still be honest about who we are. And we can teach them that, in the same way that we are here for them, they need to be there for each other.

That's what it means to be a family, a little flock wandering through the wilderness, through all the transitions and surprises that await us. A baby is born, and a person becomes a mother; another baby is born, and an only child becomes an older sister.

In the process, we all learn how to be a little bit like Moses: how to care for each other, how to be real, how to love.

17

Helping Each Other When Our Donkeys Fall

This is the secret power of being a parent: even when we're alone with our kids, we exert an invisible power over the future.

I was determined to launch back into "regular life" as soon as possible after my first child, Sylvia, was born. So determined, in fact, that when I was offered a big solo theater performance six weeks after my due date, I accepted with excitement. I couldn't imagine I wouldn't be back to normal given six whole weeks to recover from the birth. Even my mom assured me I'd be fine.

This might have been okay, except that Sylvia arrived very late, via an unexpected C-section. And so I found myself, four weeks after the birth, enduring a grueling commute as Aaron drove me over the pothole-riddled highways from Brooklyn to Manhattan for daily rehearsals.

He'd pull up at the theater's busy intersection; I'd collect Sylvia from her car seat and carry her inside while he parked the car. Then he'd come in to bounce tiny Sylvia in the empty theater while my director and I worked, occasionally stopping for a nursing break. Throughout all of this I popped Tylenol and tried to ignore the ache and tug in my C-section wound.

While I did love being back in the theater, it didn't take long to realize I'd made a mistake. I'd never had major surgery before, not to mention a baby; I hadn't realized how the first six weeks or so would be entirely different from any other time in life, or how much time and space I would need to heal.

The second time around, I structured my postpartum months very differently. When I was offered a (different) fancy performance opportunity one month after my due date, I politely declined. I worried that I might regret it, but I didn't, not a bit. Instead, I appreciated every moment of those first few postpartum months, nursing baby Elijah under the grape arbor in our backyard, rocking him to sleep in my arms as the sun fell below the horizon.

From that quiet vantage point I could see that, blissful as my little home was, the world outside was in turmoil. The news was full of systemic injustice and environmental destruction: forest fires, melting glaciers, police brutality, discrimination. I remember holding my swaddled baby and looking out my bedroom window at bees nuzzling lavender in my garden while a radio announcer described that season as "an overwhelming summer of discontent."

How, I wondered, could I reconcile these realities? On the one hand, the intimate, beautiful summer at home, gathering wildflowers with my sprite-like daughter, nursing my newborn son. On the other hand, the news full of war, oppression, and violence.

How can I balance the need for so much healing in the world with my responsibilities as a mother? How can I act justly in an unjust world?

The Torah recognizes this as a fundamental human question. Just before it starts drawing to a close, we find a flurry of specific *mitzvot*, "commandments," offering practical advice on how to do our part while we're here.

This section of the Torah always reminds me of parents dropping their teenager off at college, trying to get in some last-minute advice before the kid goes off into the world. Admittedly, some of this ancient advice is unlikely to apply in the course of our own daily lives—like the punishment for a woman who, while fighting with a man, grabs his genitals (!). Other laws seem straight-up wrong to contemporary progressive values, like the prohibition against wearing clothes of the other gender.

But when we look past those that no longer speak to us, many of these ancient laws are surprisingly relevant. They offer evergreen truths: simple, eternal prescriptions for living a good life and building a compassionate society.

Like this: "If you see someone's donkey fall down on the road, help them lift it back up" (Deuteronomy 22:4).

Or: "When you gather the harvest, don't go back and pick up what you've missed. Instead, leave it for those who need food" (Leviticus 23:22).

Or this: "If you hire a worker, pay them on the day the work is done. Don't make them wait" (Deuteronomy 24:15).

Or: "Respect the rights of the stranger, for you were strangers in the land of Egypt" (Exodus 22:20, among others).

That summer, nursing my infant on the cream-colored rocker while my toddler played on the floor, I sometimes felt cut off from the greater world. But this is the secret power of being a parent: even when we're alone with our kids, we exert an invisible power over the future. If we teach our children kindness and fairness, as the Torah's simple yet profound laws encourage, we help build the world they will live in after we're gone.

I am proud to raise my little ones as Jews. Proud that they are expected to engage with this messy world, encouraged to follow the commandments that ring true to their minds and souls. I hope that Judaism will be part of how they learn kindness, justice, and compassion. I hope my own daily actions can be a model for them. I try to learn alongside them: To help each other when our donkeys fall. To take what we need, and leave the rest for others. To treat each other fairly and with kindness. To be humble when we have power, and strong when we are powerless.

And to find meaning in our lives—in our tradition, in our families, in the work we do in the world, and in our love for one another.

18

Reading the Tenth Plague Is Different as a Mom

Now the words "slaying of the firstborn" fill me with real terror.
I have a powerful urge to go hug my own firstborn tight.

P re-motherhood, the ten plagues always felt distant, like a fairy tale. Magical, yes; creepy, yes; but not personally threatening.

Now, though, the words "slaying of the firstborn" fill me with real terror. Reading the Torah's description of what went down that night, I have a powerful urge to go hug my own firstborn tight:

> In the middle of the night Adonai struck down all the firstborn in the land of Egypt, from the firstborn of Pharaoh who sat on the throne to the firstborn of the captive who was in the dungeon, and all the firstborn of the cattle. . . . There was a loud cry in Egypt; for there was no house where there was not someone dead. (Exodus 12:29–30)

With my newly vulnerable mom-heart, I can hardly bear to think about the magnitude of this loss for the Egyptian parents. Obviously, no family deserves this, and I have to imagine that a few of these Egyptian families would have been sympathetic to the Israelite cause, perhaps even risking their own lives to protect them. Yet even their children were not spared.

So what are we—as parents, or just as compassionate people in general—supposed to do with this story?

Jewish tradition has a few suggestions for us.

First, there is the idea that we should not rejoice over an enemy's pain. Full disclosure: Some biblical stories celebrating ancient military victories definitely seem to contradict this principle. But when it comes to how we should actually live our day-to-day lives, the message is consistently in line with this teaching: "Don't rejoice when your enemies fall; don't be happy when they stumble" (Proverbs 24:17).

We reaffirm this value at the Passover seder each year. Wine is a symbol of joy, so we symbolically lessen our joy in this celebration of our Exodus. Despite the extreme oppression by Egyptian taskmasters, when we recite the ten plagues—*blood, frogs, lice, hail*—we remove a drop of wine from our glass for each one and dot it on the edge of our plate.

Phew. These are heavy themes—about losing what we most love and the price others pay for our freedom. Not exactly the vibe we associate with the Passover story, usually seen as a time of liberation and joy. As we celebrate the Exodus, we usually focus on the liberation of the Israelites after generations of oppression. And yet, reading this ancient narrative as a parent, I don't want to overlook those Egyptian mothers. As a mother myself, I feel a debt to them. In the story that's been passed down to us, their suffering brought about our freedom; because of their loss, our culture survives.

The ancient rabbis, too, took note of the human suffering in this story, and they explore it in a famous midrash. Midrash is a beautiful Jewish storytelling tradition, sort of like today's fanfic, which explores alternate retellings or side stories that could underlie biblical texts. In this classic midrash about the Exodus story, the angels rejoice as the sea closes over the Egyptians, allowing the Israelites to escape safely. But God, angry, chastises the angels: "My creatures are drowning, and you rejoice?" Even though the Egyptians have oppressed the Israelites for four hundred years, even though their defeat seems to be necessary for the Israelites' liberation, God—in the rabbis' imagination—mourns their demise.

In the midrash, this beautiful, jewel-like teaching comes from God. But I think it's really here to remind us of the complexity of being human and living in proximity to other humans—each of them like us in some ways and unlike us in others.

When the rabbis imagine God rebuking the angels, I think they are telling us not to be like Pharaoh. What is the use of our own suffering, they are saying, if it cannot teach us to have compassion for the pain of others? Soften your hearts; your children have taught you to love. Now extend that love to all the children, all the mothers, every single person in this world.

That's liberation.

19

Being Reborn in the Desert

What do we have to let go of in order to cross over into a new life?

Long ago, I went to a new-agey Passover retreat deep in the Negev desert. It was led by a hippie Jewish priestess: long hair, flowy batik dresses, lots of meditation on the schedule.

As we settled on our cushions on the first day, she explained to us that the Exodus from Egypt, which we celebrate on Passover, was actually a birth narrative. Egypt held the Israelites tightly, like a womb; then the Red Sea parted, and the Israelites passed through the narrow canal and were born anew on the other side, transformed into free people.

Now, she informed us, we were going to reenact that birth story.

We dutifully divided into pairs and stood in two lines, facing each other. Then we formed a giant human tunnel by joining our hands overhead with the person opposite us. Finally, two strong participants volunteered to carry each of us through the tunnel, one by one, so we could physically experience the Exodus. We were "birthed," one after the other, carried on our backs through a figurative Red Sea made of strangers' arms.

Though I imagine literal reenactments like this are relatively rare, understanding the Exodus as a birth narrative is a common interpretation. The Israelites are born anew as they cross the sea, leaving their familiar identities behind and heading into the unknown. Now they'll be in an entirely new place: a wilderness where they'll wander, following a cloud by day and a pillar of fire by night.

But what does it mean to be reborn when you're already an adult? What do you have to let go of in order to cross over into a new life?

As a newish mom, I'm still embarrassed to admit just how much I sometimes miss my old way of living, with its small luxuries. Sleeping in, reading the paper, watching movies on planes, folding laundry knowing it will stay folded more than ten minutes. How can I pine for those trivial things when the miracle of life is happening before my eyes? Often, I don't. But the truth is, sometimes I do. A lot.

So I am relieved to find that the Israelites seem to have similar problems letting go of their old lives—even though, unlike mine, *their* old lives were pure misery.

At first, after crossing the Sea of Reeds, the Israelites sing and dance and celebrate. But soon enough they start to grumble about desert life. First the water tastes bitter. Then they miss their delicious Egyptian meals. They even regret surviving the Exodus: "If only we had died by the hand of Adonai in the land of Egypt," they complain, "when we sat by the fleshpots, when we ate our fill of bread!" (Exodus 16:3).

In rabbinic commentary, the Israelites get a fair amount of flak for being bratty in the desert. But personally, I love this whining, because it makes me feel better about my own. Reading about the Exodus as a mom, I think one message of this story is: even if you're reborn into a miracle, it's okay to miss your old life.

There's another message that feels particularly applicable to my life right now too—about learning to ask for help.

The Israelites need a lot of support in the desert, and God gives it to them—but not until they ask for it.

They mutter about the water tasting weird; God sweetens it. They complain about missing Egyptian food; God gives them manna (which, according to tradition, tastes like whatever you want it to).

Presumably God, being omniscient, already knows what the Israelites need. But God only provides after they themselves find it within themselves to ask.

It's as if the Israelites' learning to name their own needs is the point of the story. It doesn't always come out politely, but that's natural; it's a new skill for them. As newly freed people, they have to learn to fend for themselves. The first step is identifying what they need and want; the second, having the courage to ask for it.

Moses, too, learns to ask for help in the desert. A humble person, sometimes to the point of insecurity, Moses often seems lonely, overwhelmed, and at a loss for solutions. At the end of this passage, he gets a transformative lesson in the power of community support.

The Israelites are battling another tribe; due to some biblical magic, as long as Moses holds his arms up, the Israelites win. After a while, Moses's arms get tired, and the Israelites begin to lose. Then, something surprising happens: two leaders step up to hold Moses's arms for as long as the battle takes, and in the end, the Israelites win.

The text doesn't tell us whether Moses asked for help or whether his friends simply saw the need and jumped in. I like to imagine, though, that as his triceps began to burn, as his heart pounded, as he saw the Israelites being defeated, Moses finally realized he couldn't do it alone. I like to think he turned to his friends and said, "I need you."

I admit, I was skeptical at first about that birth exercise in the desert, preparing for Passover by carrying each other through a tunnel of hands. But now I think maybe that's part of what that teacher was trying to show us. Being born, or reborn, is a messy process. And it's a lot sweeter when we carry each other, when we hold each other's hands.

20

Noah Wasn't Perfect and Neither Am I

The deeper I get into this parenting thing, the more I believe that perfection is a red herring.

I used to want to be the perfect mom. I might not have admitted it out loud, might not even have realized it, but it was true. I was determined to pick Sylvia up every single time she cried, so that she'd know she was loved. I vowed that when she grew older, I would approach her with compassion and understanding at all times, even if she misbehaved. When she started eating solid food, I'd feed her balanced, healthy, home-cooked meals every night, giving her just enough sugar so that she wouldn't freak out when she finally got a taste.

If you'd have asked me, I would have told you that I knew perfection was impossible, of course; I just wanted to do my best for my kid.

But the truth was that somewhere deep inside, I believed that if I aimed to be the perfect mom and fell short, at least I could count on landing at "pretty good."

This plan actually worked for the first few weeks of Sylvia's life. I was unfailingly cheerful, constantly appreciative of the miracle of life, a model of new motherhood.

But no one can keep that up forever. As time went on, I began to get worn down. And with each passing week, I became more of a walking disaster. I'd hear a whimper from the other room and think, *Oh no, she's crying! I must fix it immediately!* But more often than not, instead of successfully soothing Sylvia, I'd just end up crying along with her.

One day, after a particularly bad session, I took stock. Sylvia and I were both red-faced and covered in snot, and I had to admit that control was no longer an option. Aiming for perfect wasn't going to ensure I landed at "pretty good," because, as Voltaire said, "The perfect is the enemy of the good." Then again, Voltaire also said, "A witty saying proves nothing." Still, he was right: it was time to stop aiming for perfection.

(I discovered later that Voltaire was a terrible racist and antisemite. *Ugh.* This particular point of his stands, though.)

The deeper I get into this parenting thing, the more I believe that perfection is a red herring. "Good" is not a watered-down version of "perfect." It's a different animal altogether.

"Perfect" is a carefully selected selfie, airbrushed within an inch of its life. "Good" is a gorgeous, complicated, flawed, heartbreaking creature made of love and time and mistakes and forgiveness.

I'm far from the first in human history to struggle with the balance between reality and perfectionism. Just look at the story of Noah. "God saw how great humans' wickedness had become, and how every plan devised by his mind was nothing but evil all the time" (Genesis 6:5). Whoa; only ten generations after Adam and Eve wandered the Garden of Eden, we humans had already messed the whole thing up. And God's response? Well, God wanted to wipe us all out and start over with the single family on earth who had lived up to expectations.

I can't blame God for falling into this tempting trap. Perfect humans living perfect lives? What's not to like? What a dream it would be to get rid of everything unpleasant and unwished-for, and keep only the one small part of your life—let's call it "Noah" that lines up precisely with your plans.

But alas, as it turns out, even Noah's perfection is an illusion. After the world finally dries out from the massive Flood, Noah plants a vineyard, gets drunk, and holds court without his pants on—not exactly ideal behavior.

And at some point, even before that scandal, God does seem to realize that the wholesale destruction of the earth was not a good approach. God hangs a rainbow in the sky as soon as the Flood subsides and promises never to destroy the world again.

"Never again will I doom the earth because of man, since the devisings of man's mind are evil from his youth, nor will I ever again destroy every living being," God says (Genesis 8:21). God vows never to destroy the world "since the devisings of man's mind are evil"— in other words, it's precisely *because* humans are flawed that God promises to spare us in the future.

Some rabbis say that creating the world is the ultimate act of divine compassion. But I think this post-Flood vow is even more powerful. Only now, after a profound human failure, does God finally understand the complex nature of humanity, our essential imperfection. And only in giving up this dream of perfection can God finally commit to the world and to us as we truly are.

I'm not saying this is easy. It's still tempting to fantasize about the perfect life, the perfect marriage, the perfect career, the perfect version of myself as a mother. And being human, I'm sure I'll continue to slip into that fantasy.

The best I can do is to try to catch myself and remember what I'm learning from motherhood. "Perfect" is just a distraction from what's in front of us at any given moment: the arc of a rainbow, the relief of a deep breath, the sweetness of our children's small hands. What's truly important is what we see in the mirror at the end of another long day; not the perfect, but the good.

21

On the Other Side of Parental Boredom Is Awe

My kid regularly blows my mind. So how is it possible that I'm often so . . . excruciatingly . . . bored?

M y kid is anything but boring. She's a little strawberry-blond spitfire who cracks me up with her sense of humor, amazes me with her expanding grasp of language, keeps me on my toes, and regularly blows my mind.

Given all that, how is it possible that I'm often so . . . excruciatingly . . . bored?

The answer, I think, is simple. It will sound familiar to anyone who's been involved in a romantic breakup: we're just in very different places right now.

It's hard to find activities that work for both of us. Mommy and Me is cool, and we're both into baking, but there are only so many sing-alongs you can attend in a day, and if I make chocolate chip cookies four times a week I'll melt into a gooey mass.

It's not just me; we take turns being bored. Sylvia gets antsy when I spend too long in the grocery store bulk aisle. I get tired of pushing her on the swings. Sylvia finds it less than entertaining when I do dishes. I get bored singing "Old MacDonald Had a Farm" (again). And so on.

This wouldn't be such a problem if I had a healthier relationship with boredom. But I absolutely, positively hate being bored. In fact, I've spent much of my life actively running away from it, piling as many projects on my plate as possible, making sure I'm never at a loss for the next item on my to-do list.

I've long sensed that there are probably better ways to deal with boredom than sprinting in the other direction. I've suspected that my resistance to boredom means that it actually has something to teach me, and I even tried a couple of meditation retreats to help me learn its lessons. But—though I'm not proud of this—I came away from those retreats with one primary takeaway: "I'll never do *that* again."

But parenting a toddler, unlike a brief meditation retreat, is measured in months and years. And so Sylvia has become my teacher, pushing me to experiment once again with seeing boredom as a spiritual lesson rather than something to be avoided at all costs.

In fact, what I feel after a few hours at home alone with Sylvia is eerily similar to what I experienced on those meditation retreats. It's oh-so-tempting to escape this uncomfortable feeling by checking my email or cleaning the kitchen or reading a magazine or . . . doing *anything* except facing it head-on. But if I can resist that urge to escape, and instead follow my boredom to the other side, I do occasionally find a flash of something profound: the feeling of *being* rather than doing.

With all due respect to our sacred foundational text, certain sections of the Torah inspire their own share of boredom—at least on first reading. For example, as the book of Exodus winds down, we get a play-by-play of the construction of the Mishkan. Often translated as "Tabernacle," the Mishkan is a mobile sanctuary, a sacred tent in which the Israelites worship God while wandering the desert.

A brief excerpt for your enjoyment:

In the first month of the second year, on the first of the month, the Tabernacle was set up. Moses set up the Tabernacle, placing its sockets, setting up its planks, inserting its bars, and erecting its posts. He spread the tent over the Tabernacle, placing the covering of the tent on top of it—just as Adonai had commanded Moses. (Exodus 40:17–19)

Dying to hear more? Perhaps not. On the surface, this seems about as entertaining as a bookshelf assembly pamphlet. But on close reading, it becomes clear that this structure must have been stunning, especially against its stark desert setting. Blue, purple, and crimson cloths; bells of pure gold; woodworking; holy anointing oil; and magnificent priestly clothes complete with precious stones.

In addition to its visual beauty, there's something else that speaks to me as a mom. The Tabernacle is an example of the transcendence that can happen when hours and hours of human energy and repetitive tasks are devoted to a single purpose. It's a triumph of human dedication, a bit of a miracle—like a majestic cathedral built by hundreds of stonemasons over hundreds of years. Or the cumulative effect of many, many days spent nurturing a toddler and showing her that she is loved.

I may feel like I'm not doing anything important during those long afternoons with my kid, but, in fact, my loving presence (and that of her childcare providers) will resonate for the rest of her life. I once read a heartbreaking news piece about young Romanian orphans who were given food and shelter but lacked loving caregivers; into their adult lives, the orphans continued to have significantly diminished brain activity during human interactions. Infant development, scientists have learned, requires not just food, shelter, and safety, but consistent attention from caring adults. Our presence in our kids' lives is not a luxury; it's a necessity.

Hearing this in scientific language makes me suddenly, sweetly conscious of those in-between moments with my little ones, and of how each one adds up to the relationship they're developing with the world.

Building yet another tower of Duplos, I'm showing Sylvia she is loved. Walking a few steps behind her during snail-paced walks around the block, she's learning to navigate the world on her own. And fifteen minutes into pushing her on the playground swings . . . well, I'm not sure exactly what's being accomplished, and to be honest I'm definitely checking my phone by this point, but I still know that my being here is important.

Creating something awe-inspiring takes perseverance and time—whether it's weaving curtains for the Tabernacle, training for a 5K, or nurturing a young human as they learn and grow, day after day.

There's no way around it; boredom is part of the job description of being a parent. But it's also a privilege to be part of forming the most magnificent, transcendent creation of all: a human being.

Yes, I'm talking about our kids. But I'm also talking about us. We grow up alongside them, becoming more fully realized people ourselves. Hour by unglamorous hour, through the high points and the boredom alike—together, we are building something magnificent.

22
Even God Had Bad Parenting Days

It's easy to wax philosophical about impermanence.
It's much harder to access that objectivity and wisdom while
a small human is screaming at top volume.

Things are pretty confusing in my house right now. One minute Sylvia's telling me I'm her cutie pie and complimenting my earrings, and the next she's in full-on tantrum mode because I made her put on socks.

Her two-year-old emotions are mercurial, overwhelming, everything in the moment—and then suddenly they're gone. To my logical adult brain, this is frustrating. But when I'm able to get some distance, I recognize that she's also reflecting a spiritual truth: everything changes. This is the truth of impermanence, and I understand it in a new way as a mom.

Like some kind of superhero, Sylvia constantly transforms into new versions of herself. In June, she passionately declares frozen mango the most delicious fruit in the world; by July, she hates it. In the fall, she struggles to climb the play structure; by winter, she's fearlessly clambering to the top.

Even the changes change.

First there were the newborn days, which felt excruciatingly slow. During that time, if I went for a walk during what felt like hour thirty-six of the day, complete strangers on the street—who in normal times would have ignored me—would see my baby, smile ruefully, and say, "It goes so fast."

I always wanted to thwack them; nothing goes fast on four hours of sleep.

Two short years later, I couldn't believe that little tiny girl was gone forever, replaced by a walking, talking, joke-cracking toddler.

Impermanence isn't just for little ones; to be human is to exist in a state of flux. The difference is, we adults—and by "we," I mean "I"— resist change. I cling to what came before, even when it causes me suffering.

But children are masters of change. They steadily grow into new versions of themselves, letting go of who they were without a second thought. Watching them grow is a lesson in impermanence. My toddler teaches me that I, too, can change my mind. I, too, am a work in progress.

Back to real life, though. It's easy to wax philosophical about impermanence. It's much harder to actually access this level of objectivity and wisdom while a small human is screaming at top volume because you put pasta sauce on her noodles instead of next to them.

And this is why I so appreciate the fact that in the Torah, the main characters—including God—all have moments of acting like overwhelmed parents. Despite the best intentions of remaining patient and compassionate, they, like us, lose their cool.

For example, the Exodus from Egypt. We love to celebrate this story of miraculous liberation. Less often do we mention the fact that the recently liberated Israelites are extremely whiny. (Sound familiar?)

They're tired of wandering in the desert, and they sit around complaining about how they miss the delicious meat they used to eat in Egypt. Moses, like a stressed-out parent, finally hits a wall. He can't take any more whining and complains to God that he'd rather die than lead these people.

And how does God handle this? By making quail rain down from the sky, then sending a plague to kill the Israelites who choose to eat it.

This is not a pretty story. In fact, it's exactly this kind of thing that makes people think of God as a vengeful guy in the sky with a white beard.

But reading this as a mother, I think: who am I to judge? I get it. I've had my crappy parenting days too.

In the Torah, stories take place on a mythic scale. A bad day means quail raining from the sky and a deadly plague. In real life, we express our parental frustration in (hopefully) more mundane ways.

Still, I have a lot of compassion for God here, getting swept up in a difficult moment and forgetting all about patience and deep breaths. It's easy to lose it when it seems like a hard day, or a spectacular tantrum, or a difficult stage is going to last forever.

My favorite thing about this story, though, is what happens next: nothing. The Israelites keep walking, Moses stays on as their leader, and God continues to accompany them through the wilderness. In the end, this terrible episode is just a blip in their relationship.

Impermanence is in equal parts terrible and liberating. The things I love won't last forever—but the things that drive me crazy, break my heart, or just plain hurt won't last forever either. This is true in parenting, and in life.

As Sarah Napthali writes in her beautiful book *Buddhism for Mothers of Young Children*, "Impermanence, the fact that all things change, can be a mother's best friend."

Even our worst parenting moments don't last forever. No matter how rough it gets, we can always apologize. We always get another chance to wake up with our little ones and start over . . .

Until one day they're all grown up and gone, and we're the person on the street—smiling that annoying sweet smile, saying to a haggard stranger with a newborn, "Enjoy these days. It goes so fast."

23

Learning to Love Our Bodies as They Are

My body is my home, my host, my expression on this earth.
It allows me to be here with my child: to love her, to care for her.
If that's not beautiful, what is?

We tend to speak about our bodies as if they are separate from the rest of us, but that's not really how it works.

In fact, it's impossible to separate our selves from our physical forms. Our bodies are the container for everything we experience, our golden ticket to existence on this earth. We are born into them and live our lives in them, experiencing every moment through these vessels.

So it's odd, in a way, that so many of us struggle daily to love our physical selves. But it makes sense too; we all receive a constant, insidious flow of messages about "good" and "bad" aspects of our bodies.

This can be deeply serious; some of us with differing abilities, genders, sizes, and races are the target of explicit negativity and threats. Or it can be small but annoying, especially in a society where people consider it fine to comment on women's bodies.

Add in pregnancy on top of all this, and the weird bodily effects it leaves long afterward, plus the difficulty of taking care of your own physical form while taking care of a small human—and it's no surprise that many of us wrestle with accepting our bodies as new mothers.

I won't lie: I'm still working on this myself.

It's easy for me to see that other people's bodies are perfect just as they are, and harder for me to apply this to my own. But as I grow older, I am making peace with the idea that my body is absolutely beautiful, exactly as it is. It's my home, my host, my expression on this earth. It allows me to be here with my child: to love her, to care for her.

If that's not beautiful, what is?

In her book about being a hospice chaplain, *On Living*, Kerry Egan writes:

> There are many regrets and many unfulfilled wishes that patients have shared with me in the months or weeks before they die. But the time wasted hating their body, ashamed, abusing it or letting it be abused—the years, decades, or, in some cases, whole lives that people spent not appreciating their body until they were so close to leaving it—are some of the saddest.

Egan's words help me to remember the big picture: no matter what my issues are with my body right now, I will eventually part from it (or disappear along with it, or whatever the heck happens when I die). No matter how long each day feels with a toddler, I won't always be here to appreciate this body. I'd better learn to do it now, while it's here—while I'm here.

There's a Jewish holiday that resonates with this lesson too. It's called Sukkot, and it comes around every fall, when we celebrate the harvest by building a sukkah—a booth or hut made of natural materials. We're basically commanded to go on an extended camping trip in our sukkah, eating meals and even sleeping in it for a week or so.

The sukkah is, by design, an extremely simple structure: open to the elements, with a highly porous roof. While any material works for the walls, most people use lightweight, impermanent materials: plywood, canvas, sometimes even bedsheets. In other words, it usually feels more like a tent than a house. The sukkah, like the human body, is a highly impermanent, charmingly imperfect structure, which we dwell in for a while.

By temporarily moving into the sukkah's precarious shelter, open to the elements and built to last only a week or so rather than years, we remember the essential impermanence of life in this world. The sacred thinness of the walls reminds us of what it means to be cold, to feel the air on our skin. The roof of branches or bamboo, through which we must be able to see the stars, reminds us that only in this vulnerable body can we experience the universe—how very tiny and miraculous we are.

Every autumn, Sukkot invites us back into the bodily realm. For me, this has become a radical reminder of body positivity. We enter a hut made of natural materials that have grown, like our bodies, from the soil. We enter an experience of time in which obsolescence is measured in millennia, not months.

The ancient rabbis didn't frame the sukkah in terms of body positivity. But perhaps they gesture toward this idea when they point out that the sukkah is one of the only rituals in Jewish practice that require us to show up with our whole bodies (another is mikvah). And this makes so much sense. Like the sukkah, our bodies are temporary dwellings. They aren't built to last forever. We only stay here for a while, until we return to the earth.

When I've scrolled past too many airbrushed images, and I start to feel that familiar self-criticism creeping in, I try to take a deep breath and think of the sukkah. I think of Kerry Egan's words, how her patients wished not for different bodies, but rather that they'd loved their own bodies more.

My body will never be the same as it was before I became a mom. But pregnancy and birth are not the only things that have changed my body, and they certainly won't be the last. That's the deal with living in a body; as long as we're lucky enough to be alive, we are always changing.

Looking at my children, I feel such powerful love for their small forms. I hope that they can be at peace with their own bodies, whatever they may look like when they're older. And I want to model this for them.

So instead of spending my life trying to stuff this luminous flesh back into some idea of how it should look, I do my best to love my body—exactly as it is, imperfect and beautiful. My sukkah, my temporary home on this earth.

24
God of the Breast

I'd expected to feel wild, heart-bursting joy, holding this perfect, magical creature to my breast. What surprised me was that I felt closer to death than ever before.

Just after Sylvia was born, as I held her delicate, seven-pound body for the first time, I experienced two incredibly strong, contradictory feelings.

I'd expected one of these feelings: a wild, heart-bursting joy at holding this perfect, magical creature to my breast. What surprised me, as she began to nurse, was the other one: at that peak moment of holding newborn life in my arms, I felt closer to death than ever before.

Holding that little bundle, I suddenly understood my body as a vessel that had helped another being cross the line between nonexistence and existence. I had physically carried her from one side to the other. I was aware of our shared strength and our fragility. In that magical, dangerous space, I felt close to Shechinah, the feminine presence of the Divine.

Much later, reading the end of the book of Genesis, I was reminded of this wild moment.

As Genesis draws to a close, the women who have populated its stories seem to disappear. Fathers, sons, and grandfathers abound; but where are the women?

But then Jacob begins his blessing:

The God of your father who helps you,

And Shaddai who blesses you

With blessings of heaven above,

Blessings of the deep that couches below,

Blessings of the breast and womb. (Genesis 49:25)

Though this blessing begins with "God of your father," from there it dives directly into feminine language. *Blessings of the breast and womb?* I wouldn't be surprised to find that phrase in a 1970s feminist haggadah. Right on!

There's also that mysterious name Shaddai, which may also contain feminine imagery. Shaddai is one of many Jewish names for God, but no one is certain what it literally means. Some say it comes from *shadad*, meaning "to destroy"— which would align it with the aspect of God that encompasses devastation, even death.

But others point out that Shaddai sounds very similar to *shadayim*, the Hebrew word for breasts. In this interpretation, the name would refer to the feminine, life-giving, nourishing aspect of God. In other words, the "God of the Breast." Which resonates with Jacob's words: "Blessings of the breast and womb."

How can one name of God contain both of these meanings: creation and destruction, nourishment and violence? Is this tension related to the absence of women from this section of the Torah? And why do we encounter these strange juxtapositions of life and death at the end of the beginning of the Torah?

Like our holy texts, our mythical ancestors are complicated. Our revered forefather Jacob, for example, frankly had some pretty terrible parenting moments—like blatantly favoring his son Joseph.

Yet that extremely low point in biblical family relationships coexists with this beautiful scene of Jacob, on his deathbed, blessing his sons, who have reconciled and reunited.

It's all part of the same story. And these wild opposites are part of parenting as well.

Just as Jacob's blessing to his descendants includes contradictory extremes—the heaven above and the deep that couches below—our lives as parents include beginnings wrapped in endings.

Joy and heartbreak intertwine; nourishment and loss coexist. And through it all, these ancient stories guide us and hold us. They remind us that families are never perfect. That we are not the first ones on this journey, nor will we be the last.

That divine blessing resides not only in the stories of fathers and sons, but in the bodies of mothers too.

That it's all woven together. Masculine and feminine, breast and womb, blood and milk, creation and destruction, the beginning of the end and the end of the beginning.

PART 3

The Everyday Sacred

Parenting as *Tikun*

25

It's Hard to Honor Your Father and Mother When You're in the Terrible Twos

What does honoring your father and mother even mean for a toddler who refuses to share her sandbox shovel with her best friend?

As a baby, Sylvia was extra sweet in the early morning.

We had a predictable, adorable routine: she'd wake up in her crib and coo, then cry, until one of us came over to pick her up. When she saw our faces looming over her crib, she'd break into a huge smile and start pedaling the air with glee. Once she could stand up, she'd grip the sides of the crib and call to us until one of us walked into her room (which was really a walk-in closet). "Mama!" or "Papa!" she'd yell, in pure delight, like an adorable little tiger in her cage. We'd lift her up into our arms and feel that oxytocin rush that got us through the day, tired as we were.

On the morning of her second birthday, Sylvia woke up, talked to herself for a while as usual, then called out "Mama, Papa!" I slid open her door and threw her a giant smile, ready to drink in her morning love and adore her in return. I was excited to show her the purple streamers I'd taped up to the ceiling in honor of her birthday.

But something had changed.

As soon as she saw me, Sylvia stood up in her crib, gripped the bars, and screamed, for the first time ever: "Go *away*, Mama!"

Terrible twos, right on schedule.

I explained that "Go away" isn't nice; I offered a cup of orange juice. And just like that, I was back in Sylvia's good graces. As she toddled past our bed to the kitchen, I exchanged glances with Aaron, who raised his eyebrows in that complicated but frequent look we seemed to pass back and forth constantly since becoming parents—a combination of "We're screwed" and "This is hilarious."

"Honor your father and mother," the Torah tells us, "so that you may live long in the land God is giving you" (Exodus 20:12). I'd always related to that particular commandment from my own point of view as a daughter. Now, it was my turn to be the mother.

Honoring our parents is not just a helpful suggestion; it's one of the Ten Commandments. And though it sounds simple, the rabbis consider it one of the hardest commandments to observe fully.

Consider the passage of the Talmud where the rabbis obsess about what behavior, exactly, defines honoring one's parents. They consider their own behavior as examples. When Rabbi Avimi brought his father a glass of water only to find that his father had fallen asleep, he stood there waiting, holding the glass, until his father woke up. This, the rabbis agree, is a good start.

Then they consider Rabbi Tarfon, who allowed his mother to use his body as a step stool to get in and out of bed every day. Sounds pretty good to me, but the rabbis proclaim this isn't even half of the honor he should be showing her.

Finally, Rabbi Yochanan chimes in to say he considers himself lucky to have been orphaned at birth so he doesn't have to try to fulfill this impossible mitzvah!

I hope my kids are nice to me when they grow up (though I don't want them to let me use them as step stools!). But as the mother of a two-year-old, I have to wonder: what does honoring your father and mother even mean for a toddler who refuses to share her sandbox shovel with her best friend?

As usual, it's all about balance. I have a responsibility to understand where my daughter is developmentally, while also teaching her to be kind and respectful, even at this young age. Being a generally sensitive human, I have to admit an involuntary flinch when my child sneers, "Go away, Mama!" But I also know that this isn't something to worry about. She's just doing her job as a self-respecting two-year-old. These little explosions are "developmentally appropriate"—clinical language for "It's cool; this, too, shall pass."

And, for better or worse, this is just the beginning. As her parents, Aaron and I are on the front line of her growing heart and mind. Like every human, she's going to have to learn how to negotiate the daily mess of life. She'll have to figure out how to manage her emotions. And as often as not, if we're doing our jobs, we'll be right there to absorb (or gracefully dodge) the blows.

Do I want to teach my kid about honoring her parents? Yes. But at this point in her life, a lecture about mitzvot would be utterly ridiculous. So, what's a toddler parent to do?

Age-appropriate expectations are always good. Beyond that, I think all I can do is lead by example. Which means it's up to me and Aaron to show Sylvia how to honor people—her mother and father, yes, and also everyone on the planet.

As she gets older, she'll be watching how I interact with my own parents. She'll be watching how Aaron and I treat each other, and how we treat her.

And she'll also be watching how we treat ourselves. I want her to see me treat myself with patience and kindness. To give myself a few more minutes of rest sometimes, as Rabbi Avimi did with his father. To support myself through transitions, as Rabbi Tarfon did with his mother.

To love and honor *myself* as her mother, in hopes that when she's old enough, she'll do the same.

26

My Toddler's Just Not That into Me

We're going to mess up, going to break rules, going to lose our tempers. But we can always find our way back to each other.

Parenting a toddler is a whiplash journey of highs and lows. One moment Sylvia radiates utter joy and unbearable cuteness, like her spontaneous exclamation one night of "Thank you, Mama, for brush my teeth!" The next morning she's committed to her despair, "Orange juice pleeeeease!" she shouts, but when I bring her some, she wails, "No, *apple* juice!" and bursts into tears.

Adorable as she is, riding an emotional roller coaster is not a particularly sustainable way to live—even if it's developmentally appropriate. I often find myself wondering how to balance the extremes of this experience: on the one hand, acknowledging the miraculous parts without glossing over the day-to-day difficulties; on the other, acknowledging the challenges without getting sucked into negativity.

One great help in my journey to understand what the hell is going on, and get through the day, has been a very old series of parenting books.

This series, by child psychologist Louise Bates Ames (1908–1996), was written over forty years ago. But reading it, I felt like the author was speaking directly to me. Her books are structured around each year of life—*Your One-Year-Old, Your Two-Year-Old, Your Three-Year-Old*—and each one goes deep into the world of that particular part of childhood, as well as parenting.

Around Sylvia's second birthday, I checked *Your Two-Year-Old* out of our local library. It's an unsentimental book, distinctly different from most contemporary parenting advice. It's not sweet and cheerleadingy and "you-got-this, mama"; instead, Ames matter-of-factly describes the behaviors I'm witnessing, acknowledges that some of them totally suck from a parent's perspective, helps me understand why they're happening, and suggests ways of dealing with it.

Reading *Your Two-Year-Old*, I also felt oddly reminded of a very different handbook on human relationships that had helped me at a very different time in my life: a little hot-pink book published in 2004 called *He's Just Not That into You*, by Greg Behrendt and Liz Tuccillo.

That book was inspired by a famous *Sex and the City* episode in which Miranda (a no-nonsense lawyer) tries to decipher the mysterious behavior of a guy she's dating. Sometimes he fawns over her, sometimes ignores her; Miranda and her best friend, Carrie, stumped by this inconsistency, spend hours analyzing his every move.

Finally, Carrie's boyfriend, Jack Berger, overhears them and bluntly solves the mystery. "He's just not that into you," Berger tells Miranda. At first she's offended, but then she realizes he's offering her a gift: liberation. She's been wasting precious energy trying to parse a potential partner's interest or intentions when she should probably just walk away and live her life.

He's Just Not That into You expanded on this revelation. Its authors sold a ton of books by offering straightforward advice for people dating in the early internet age, with its confusing, still-being-written rules about when to text back and what to say. Their core suggestion was simple: if someone is unclear about their intentions, or treats you like crap, or even *sort of* like crap, don't spend hours rehashing every message. Just assume they're not that into you, and let it go.

It's odd to compare raising a toddler to internet dating, and yet reading *Your Two-Year-Old*, I, too, felt liberated. I suddenly saw that, like Miranda in *Sex and the City*, I'd been stuck in an unhelpful communication cycle—though instead of pining over a fickle suitor, I'd been dealing with my own toddler's confusing cycle of adoration, frustration, and obliviousness. (Other parallels between toddler life and dating life include sleep deprivation, boring my friends with minutiae, and waking up to find someone staring at me.)

Just when I thought I was done with romantic drama, here I was, facing the same truths in parenting that I'd had to learn in dating. Basic stuff, like how to maintain a cool head in the face of unpredictability. How to not take things personally. How to stop myself from wondering: does this person even *like* me?

Reading *Your Two-Year-Old*, just like *He's Just Not That into You* had years before, helped me see a truth I couldn't quite access through meditation, therapy, and endless conversations. Sometimes other people are just doing their thing. It's not personal. It's not about me.

Sure, I was already aware, intellectually, that my toddler's behavior is not about me. But really *knowing* this was another thing. It feels natural to melt with adoration and pride at the cute moments, and to collapse into frustration and self-criticism during the hard ones. And yeah, I wouldn't be human if I didn't get pissed off sometimes.

But in general, I just have to take a step back and give both of us some space.

This wisdom is echoed in the Torah—another, much older, still-best-selling collection of advice that can help us regain perspective on difficult days. Full of stories and rules about how to live a good life, our sacred book is also very clear on the fact that we humans are complicated. We have mysterious, innate drives. We are going to want to do all sorts of wild things, some of which will hurt other people. So the Torah gives us the holiday of Yom Kippur, which openly acknowledges these flaws, then offers forgiveness—because none of us is going to be our best self all the time.

We're going to mess up, going to break rules, going to lose our tempers. But we can always find our way back to each other—and back to ourselves.

Your Two-Year-Old, He's Just Not That into You, the Torah. Reading these very different texts side by side, all three seem to guide me toward that middle ground. It's a calm place, where we can take a step back from the ups and downs of life. Where we can acknowledge the miraculous parts without glossing over rough ones, and acknowledge the daily challenges without dwelling in negativity. Where we can remember that any given moment is part of a much bigger story.

And that even on difficult days, at its core, parenting is a love story.

27
Our Messy Temples

Having a kid is like going to school—but for spiritual lessons rather than practical knowledge.

Y ou know how in communal-living situations, there's often a messy housemate—the one who provokes the neat roommates to hang chore wheels on the fridge and Post-its reading "*Please* do your dishes" over the sink? I confess: that was me. I've just always been . . . a bit of a slob.

But motherhood has taught me that although my cleanliness standards may be low, they do, in fact, exist. Who knew?

As it turns out, I prefer my couch cushions paint-free, I would rather liquids stay in their cups, and I am driven to distraction by uncapped markers and Lego-strewn floors.

This results in a few uncomfortable feelings. Among them: a sudden empathy for my housemates over the years, a sense of remorse for my past messes, and a raging desire to control my current space.

I've been thinking about it, and I've narrowed my options down to two choices. I can continue striving for control over my living space. This option entails my being pissed off all the time because there is a Lego permanently imprinted on my heel and Cheerios encrusted on the stairs. Bonus results: waking up upset, going to bed angry.

Or I can accept that control is not an option right now. This requires my expecting mess and physical discomfort, and realizing that this is temporary. Bonus results: acceptance, maybe even some peace.

The truth is, this is not just about my living room. It's about my body—which I'm finally realizing will never really "bounce back." It's about my work—which I still love as much as ever but just can't approach with the same utter single-mindedness as before. It's about doing something I swore I would never do: lowering my standards.

Once again, my children are my teachers. Sometimes I think having a kid is like going to school, but for spiritual lessons rather than practical knowledge. Or maybe it's more like *leaving* school for the real world after graduation. All those rules and worksheets and grades that once loomed large suddenly seem meaningless when you're faced with Real Life.

Because Real Life, especially with kids, is not a place of perfection or neatness. It's rarely calm or orderly. It's hectic, and loud, and strewn with uncapped markers.

The rabbis of the Talmud must have known this—when were little kids ever neat and orderly?—and yet they compare our homes to the ancient Temple. "When the Temple stood," the rabbis say, "the altar provided atonement. Now, the [home] table offers atonement." In other words, home is the place where we meet the Divine.

In the Torah, the ancient Temple is a place reserved for perfection. Priests with any physical differences or disabilities are excluded from offering sacrifices, and animals with any blemishes or injuries, likewise, cannot be offered.

Reading this through modern eyes is disturbing. Seriously, a disabled priest is not qualified to make communal offerings to God? Wouldn't priests with disabilities or physical differences have *more* compassion and wisdom than some strapping young guy who's never been sick a day in his life?

Here's the catch: These rules no longer apply. Jews haven't offered sacrifices for almost two thousand years, since the Romans destroyed the Temple in Jerusalem, where all of this once took place.

In other words, perfection is over.

So now, when I think about all those rules about perfect priests, I wonder . . . maybe the destruction of the Temple wasn't just an accident of history (or an expression of divine anger, as some people think). Maybe a place that emphasized perfection could never last in this imperfect world. Maybe it had to be replaced by our imperfect homes. And maybe the priests had to be replaced by us parents.

After all, becoming a mother is not unlike signing up for a religious sect, with its strange rules and daily schedule, its spiritual highs and lows, its minutiae and mysteries. And like the priests, we parents have a sacred workplace, the center of our rituals: our homes.

According to tradition, the Temple's sanctity lives on in our very own kitchens and living rooms and bedrooms.

So, instead of priests in robes, here we are: parents in rumpled T-shirts, stained with our kids' breakfast. And instead of the sacrificial fires and animal offerings those priests used to perform on behalf of the Israelites, here's our work: the meals we prepare, the floors we sweep, the little clothes we wash over and over, the bedtime songs we sing quietly at night.

But ours is not a priesthood of perfection. Quite the opposite.

Our sacred service is about showing up exactly as we are, and about finding deeper ways to love our children and ourselves, imperfections and all.

This is where true holiness is: right in front of our eyes, among the tantrums and spilled juice and the parenting mistakes.

Right in the middle of our messy temples.

28
The Transformative Powers of Bath Time

The Torah takes grossness in stride; it's just part of being human.

For a holy book, the Torah certainly has a lot to say about skin conditions. For example, there are two whole chapters in the book of Leviticus dealing with scaly skin, "greenish streaks," and "eruptive affections."

This sounds pretty weird, but I also relate to it personally. Having dealt with acne for much of my life, I am intimately acquainted with the fact that it's hard not to obsess when our bodies do something weird, even if it's "just cosmetic."

So I appreciate that the Torah doesn't focus on the "eruptive affections" themselves. Instead, it shows us how to move past them. This passage takes the grossness in stride; it seems to accept that this is just part of being human. Instead of freaking out, it gives us a long list of instructions about what to do when our bodies suddenly erupt into weirdness. How to heal, how to return to ourselves and to the community, how to refocus on the holiness of our bodies.

The Torah's recommendations vary, but there are a few common elements: a priest, a period of separation from the community, some sort of sacrifice or offering. And at the end of this process, there's almost always an immersion in sacred waters.

Which brings me to the modern, kid-focused version of this ancient tradition: bath time.

Most evenings around seven Sylvia enters the tub covered in the evidence of a toddler day well spent. You know the look: pasta sauce in her curls, dried snot on her cheek, dirt on her knees, lint between her toes, streaks of green finger paint in random places.

Twenty minutes later, after gentle scrubbing with some over-priced "natural baby" soap and a washcloth, a very different Sylvia emerges from the bathtub. Wrapped up in a giant hooded towel, she glows with cleanness, from her curls down to her little toes.

My toddler doesn't need a priest, a separation, or a sacrifice to clean off the mud, marker, and dried juice. All she needs is the last step, her ritual 7:00 p.m. immersion. It's a physical cleaning, but it's more than that: a bath signifies that the day is coming to an end, that we're winding down and preparing for bedtime.

On normal days, a ritual shower is enough for me to feel renewed too. But for larger transitions of the body—giving birth, or recovering from a major illness, or maybe even just the end of a menstrual period, as the Torah describes—this ancient tradition of immersion continues to this day in the ongoing tradition of mikvah, the ritual bath.

Every city with a Jewish community has a mikvah, and in places without an official one, immersing in any natural water source is considered kosher. And people go to great lengths to keep this commandment; I have a friend whose great-great-grandmother, a Russian Jew who immigrated to South Dakota, would have her daughter break through the frozen river with an ax so she could immerse!

In contemporary Jewish life, some mikvahs are run very traditionally, only allowing immersion at specific times by members of the community—for example, before getting married, or when a married woman ends her period each month, or as part of a conversion ceremony. Increasingly, cities also have "community mikvahs." These are open, progressive spaces that invite people to honor any passages for which they feel called to immerse: bat mitzvah, coming out as queer or trans, or divorce.

The mikvah is a powerful spiritual tool, harnessing the element of water and its symbolic energy of rebirth and transformation. It's not necessarily for everyday immersion, though. For that purpose, I have what I think of as my "home mikvah." The same bathtub where my kid gets clean each night offers me a gateway to my own small, private ritual of healing and reconnecting with myself.

After Sylvia goes to bed, after the house is as clean as it's going to get and I've finished whatever work I can squeeze out, I love to run a grown-up bath, as hot as I can stand it, with candles and essential oils, and the lights turned low. It's my way of tapping into the profound power of the ritual bath: letting go of the day, coming to a place of peace and gratitude for my body.

I love how this simplest of rituals—lowering my body into water—has its roots in ancient traditions. I love how it connects me to people across time who have also relaxed their tired, sacred bodies into the water, letting go. Finally, after a long day of nurturing others, taking some time to nurture ourselves.

I am grateful for these sacred water rituals, whether in a community mikvah, a natural body of water, or simply a bathtub. They offer us rest, relaxation, healing. They help us appreciate life in these bodies we are given. They help us move past the grosser side of physical existence, reminding us that our bodies are holy, and beautiful, no matter what.

29

How Some Sexy Vibes Saved the Jewish People

Like Pharaoh, I impose unreasonable demands—on myself.

I n some parts of the Torah, there's not a mother to be found. But in the first chapters of the book of Exodus, mothers are everywhere. And though their stories aren't always front and center, according to rabbinic commentators, they're the stars of the show.

The story starts out with a big bad father figure: a new Pharaoh, who hates the Israelites and decides to destroy them.

This momentous decision sets into motion a series of events, all of which are led by women. There's Moses's birth mother, who sends him off in a basket of reeds to save his life. And Moses's sister, Miriam, who watches over him as he floats down the Nile. And Pharaoh's own daughter, who rescues baby Moses from the water and becomes his adoptive mom.

These are the celebrity moms of Exodus. But standing behind them are the regular, unnamed mothers who make the whole story possible.

These women can briefly be spotted in the text but are more a major presence in the Midrash, the ancient rabbinic stories that explore the "story behind the story" of biblical texts. According to one midrash, women are the only reason the Israelites survived their enslavement in Egypt. In this version of the story, Pharaoh plans to destroy the Israelites by making the men work so hard that they are too exhausted to go home and sleep with their wives. No sex, no babies, no next generation of Israelites.

But Pharaoh has not accounted for the women's resilience, or their determination to keep their tribe alive. So despite their enslavement, the women devise an ingenious plan to catch and sell fish, then use the money to buy wine. They invite their husbands out into the orchards, drink and flirt with them under the trees, and make sure to take it all the way. Nine or so months later . . . Jewish babies!

According to the rabbis, these Israelite women—and their ability to create sexy vibes under terrible circumstances—are literally responsible for Jewish survival. (No, the rabbis do not use the term "sexy vibes.")

When his plan fails, Pharaoh's focus shifts from conception to birth, and another pair of women rises up to resist. In his genocidal plan B, Pharaoh commands the Egyptian midwives to kill all boys born to Israelite women. But these two midwives bravely defy him. They let the babies live; then, they tell Pharaoh that the Israelite women are so quick in their labor that the midwives can't even get there in time to deliver the babies.

(Sidenote: I now know this superfast delivery is a real thing, called "precipitous labor"—the woman who shared my postpartum hospital room had it, and I heard her tell her story over and over to visiting relatives. In the story of the midwives, though, precipitous labor is just the cover; it's actually the midwives' heroism that saves the baby boys.)

As a mom, I feel personally connected to these stories about women and babies. But I also relate to Pharaoh's plan C, which is directed instead toward the Israelite men.

If Pharaoh can't stop the Israelites from procreating and giving birth, he decides, he'll break the men's spirits. He increases their already staggering workload, requiring them not only to make bricks but also to gather the straw themselves, with no reduction in the number of bricks they had to make, adding hours of work every day. He's trying to work them to death with the simple tyranny of impossible expectations.

Let me pause for a moment and acknowledge that in a world where physical enslavement still exists, I'm grateful to be a free person. At the same time, we are encouraged to read our stories as metaphors for emotional experiences—and I relate to more than one side of this story.

Like Pharaoh, I impose unreasonable demands—on myself. To do as much as I did before adding kids into the mix. To get as much work done, and as well; to keep a relatively tidy house; to show up as a friend; to show up as a partner. And the way our society is set up plays the role of a Pharaoh here, too, failing to support parents structurally and economically.

So, like the Israelite brickmakers facing endless work, sometimes I'm exhausted. Sometimes, something has to give.

Maybe we can learn from this story to control what we can: to be gentler with ourselves during the early years of straw gathering.

We can't necessarily change the structures that hold us, but we can lower our own expectations. We can consciously decide not to stress over dishes in the sink, order takeout burritos for dinner more often, give our kids screen time on weekend mornings so we can sleep in. We can also set limits on what we add on, from volunteer requests to extra projects at work.

Learning to say "no" is a way to de-Pharaohize our inner lives.

This is especially important because all of Pharaoh's plans are interconnected. The tyranny of impossible expectations leads back to Pharaoh's plan A, the destruction of our most intimate relationships. Whether romantic partners or just close friends, we need each other. If we're all exhausted from unsustainable lives, who's going to sell the fish to buy the wine to keep the love alive?

So I take these lessons from the women of Exodus: Have reasonable expectations of yourself. Be gentle with yourself. Be strong. And—when it's time—don't forget the sexy vibes.

30
Remaining Calm in the Face of Uncertainty

To someone like me, blessed with an anxiety-prone mind, living with uncertainty does not come naturally. My tendency toward catastrophic thinking is as strong as it is unhelpful.

R ecently, my adorable Sylvia has developed a disturbing new habit: pulling her friends' hair. She'll be happily playing with another kid at the park on a sunny day, a calm and bucolic scene. Then, without warning, she'll grab her playmate's curls, shriek in excitement, and yank with all her might.

The first time it happened, I couldn't help worrying: was this the beginning of a real problem?

So I did what any mother would: consulted Dr. Google. Who, thankfully, told me it was just a stage. I even discovered one pediatrician who goes so far as to arrange playdates between his little patients who like to pull hair and bite. (Apparently, they mutually attack each other, realize it sucks, and stop forever.)

"Just a stage." Reading these words, my whole body relaxes. But it also makes me conscious of how often we only get part of the picture as parents, and how hard it is to stay calm when we don't have all the information.

Whether it's an infant with a fever in the middle of the night, a developmental milestone we're waiting for anxiously, an attack-dog toddler, or whatever karmic horrors await me in the teenage years, so much of parenting consists of wondering: is this just a passing phase, or is this forever?

Sometimes a doctor or a book or internet search can set our minds at ease. Often, though, there's nothing we can do but wait and see. And in the meantime, we need to learn to live with that uncertainty.

To someone like me, blessed with an anxiety-prone mind, living with uncertainty does not come naturally. My tendency toward catastrophic thinking is as strong as it is unhelpful. When something vaguely disturbing happens, the thought is so real I can almost hear it: "This could be the beginning of the end!" That voice is just a future projection, not reality—but I have to remain on guard so as not to just fall into instinctively believing it. In a way, that voice is tempting. Sort of like . . . Satan.

We often think of Satan as a Christian construct, but Satan exists in Judaism too—appearing in the Talmud, for example, as a trickster who likes to mess with God by convincing humans to doubt. And one of Satan's favorite tricks to play on us is catastrophic thinking.

For example, the profoundly troubling story of God commanding Abraham to offer up his son, Isaac. Though God changes the plan and Isaac is not sacrificed, the fact that it seems to *almost* happen is very disturbing. Also disturbing is the fact that Sarah, Isaac's mother, is not included in the narrative. Where is she while her son is almost sacrificed on a mountain? The Torah doesn't say.

The rabbis notice, though, that the very next chapter of the Torah begins with Sarah's death. They take this juxtaposition and run with it, writing midrashim (rabbinic storytelling traditions) to fill in the gap between the two stories. And that's where the rabbis insert Satan.

In their version, Satan sees how bad the optics of Abraham's actions are, and takes this opportunity to visit Sarah and whisper some catastrophic thinking into her ear. Satan shows her a vision of her husband holding a knife over their son, implying that Abraham has gone through with the sacrifice. Shocked and grieved, Sarah's soul flies out of her body and she dies—which means that she isn't there to welcome Isaac when he does, in fact, return from the mountain alive.

Seen this way, Sarah's death offers us a wildly extreme version of what can happen when potentially troubling information causes us to assume the worst-case scenario. Even though my own moments of uncertainty are thankfully much less terrifying than Sarah's, they still feel huge in the moment. Like on the playground the other day, when my inner Satan was shrieking, "Your kid pulled that poor kid's hair . . . By the time she's fifteen she'll be pulling knives on her friends!" That's how anxiety works: it magnifies reasonable concerns into giant shadow monsters.

I told a wise mom friend about Sylvia's hair pulling, and she suggested a phrase for me to say, firmly but gently, while deflecting my daughter out of attack mode: "I'm going to stop you from pulling kids' hair until you can stop yourself."

I love how this sentence says everything in one small, beautiful package: "I trust and expect you to learn to control your behavior, but until then, I'm here to help guide you. One day, you'll be able to do it on your own."

As I began to use this phrase with Sylvia, I realized that I can also use it on myself, to help myself learn to live with uncertainty. When I can't see what's around the corner, when my mind wants to jump to the worst possible outcome, just like Sarah did, picturing the death of her beloved son at her own husband's hand, I can tell myself, gently but firmly: "I'm going to stop you from worrying until you can stop yourself."

Or, if that doesn't work, I can always go all out and whisper, "Not today, Satan."

31

Tantrums, Talking Donkeys, and Weather

Living with a toddler is a reminder that there are invisible forces at play. Whether we call them God, emotions, magnetic fields, angels, or brain waves; they're there.

Ah, tantrums. One of the great mysteries of parenting. They're like little tornadoes that suddenly touch down at inconvenient times, leaving the room covered in snot and tears. Like Auntie Em in the storm cellar, there's not much you can do except wait out the storm.

Still, you have to do *something* while you wait. So I am thrilled to announce that I have developed a new strategy for this. I call it, "Nodding and saying, 'Okay.'"

How it works is simple: I don't deny Sylvia's powerful emotions. But I don't give them a ton of oxygen, either. Instead, I watch her calmly and say, quietly, "Okay." This means, "I'm going to take a step back and compassionately watch you flail for now. I trust this little storm will be over soon. And if it's a real issue, we can deal with it later."

Bonus: this strategy works for getting through my own adult freak-outs too!

It also works at the opposite end of the spectrum, when my kid is distracted by joy. It's a familiar situation: we're late for a playdate, I'm trying to get her to hustle for those last two blocks—and instead, she stops every ten feet or so, enraptured by a potato bug, or a fallen blossom, or a splotch of gum on the sidewalk.

Toddler parenting is all about those detours. And whether the detour is joy or a tantrum, right now my life is all about nodding and saying, "Okay." The lessons in patience and compassion just keep coming—lessons that remind me of the Torah's story of Balaam and his donkey.

Balaam is a foreign prophet. He's riding his donkey on his way to visit the Israelites, but the donkey keeps swerving and stopping, apparently for no reason.

Actually, there is a reason: the donkey keeps seeing an angel sent by God to stop Balaam from cursing the Israelites. It is swerving and stopping to avoid the angel. But because Balaam can't see the angel, he thinks his donkey is randomly acting out. Annoyed, Balaam beats the donkey, at which point she begins talking (!) to explain her side of the story.

As a mom, I get Balaam's frustration. (Though he's the villain of the story, this isn't the first time my mom-life has me identifying with the bad guy.) It's annoying to be constantly waylaid by detours and distractions, whether by a toddler or a donkey—especially when there's no perceptible reason they're happening.

But even though Balaam thinks he's in charge and that his donkey is being ridiculous, just as I think I'm in charge and Sylvia's being silly, we are both mistaken. In both of these situations, something invisible is happening. In Balaam's story, it's an angel sent by God; in my case, it's my daughter's passions, desires, hunger, and exhaustion.

Living with a toddler, like the story of Balaam, is a reminder that there are invisible forces at play. Whether we call them God, emotions, magnetic fields, angels, or brain waves; they're there. As an adult, it's all too easy to be like Balaam, rolling my eyes at the inconvenience of this mystery. But little kids are attuned to the invisible.

Whether this attunement manifests in an inexplicable refusal to put on shoes, or a blissed-out, five-minute sidewalk detour, I can't force my toddler to ignore what captures her emotions and imagination. I can only nod, say "Okay," and wait it out.

And, on a good day, I can let her inspire me to pay more attention to the invisible—to notice my own emotions, nourish my own imagination, and open my heart a little bit more to the mysteries that surround us.

32
Even Moses Needed Some Time Off

We've all been pushed past our limits, to a place where the calm, nurturing version of ourselves feels completely out of reach.

P ardon my French, but for a great leader, Moses certainly loses his shit a surprising number of times in the Torah.

One of his most famous public meltdowns is the moment when he loses control and, in a quest to find water, hits a rock instead of speaking to it.

The children of Israel, recently liberated from Egypt, have been whining nonstop; now they're complaining that they're thirsty. Tired of their incessant noise, Moses complains to God, who says, "Speak to this rock, and water will come out" (Numbers 20:8).

But instead of speaking, Moses hits the rock. Twice.

As a mom, I can relate. We've all been pushed past our limits, to a place where the calm, nurturing version of ourselves feels completely out of reach.

Thinking about this moment in Moses's life, I wish I could go back in time to just before this incident and give Moses a gift certificate for whatever the prophetic equivalent of a massage might be. "Take the afternoon off," I want to tell him. "I got this." Because the result of his adult tantrum is grave: as punishment, God says Moses will not live to enter the Promised Land.

Taken literally, this story is a giant bummer on all levels. First Moses loses it, then God's punishment appears to be way out of proportion. Could God, too, have been pushed past some limit? When we read about Moses hitting the rock and being punished, are we just witnessing a cycle of fed-up behavior that escalates to the highest levels? The whole thing feels intrinsically unfair to me.

But, as one of my teachers in yeshiva used to say, "The gates of interpretation are always open"—which I take to mean that I can't change the outcome of stories I don't like, but I can change the way I read them.

In this case, I wonder if there's something about Moses hitting the rock rather than speaking to it—the harshness, even violence, of this action—that represents a judgmental impulse we all struggle with, not only toward the world, but toward ourselves.

Perhaps speaking gently to ourselves, rather than metaphorically hitting ourselves, would be a powerful move for all of us.

This metaphor of hitting ourselves resonates with one of the traditions of Yom Kippur, when we literally beat our own breasts. During the confessional prayers, we have a tradition of making a fist and knocking against our heart with each sin we list. This is a physical symbol that the hurt we've caused actually causes us pain too.

Some people in synagogue bang their chests emphatically, as if they're trying to show how serious they are. But a wise teacher of mine once suggested that instead, we try tapping our hearts gently, as if to say, "Wake up—I know you're in there, and I love you." This is both a gentler and more effective way of bringing ourselves back to our best selves. Out of love, rather than anger; tapping, rather than striking.

That emphatic chest-banging some people do on Yom Kippur reminds me of Moses hitting the rock. It also reminds me, on a more personal level, of how often I'm tempted to judge myself against some ideal mother, and even to judge my kid against some ideal kid. But we're not ideal; we're real. Flawed, complicated, full of love, and sometimes very whiny—just like Moses and the Israelites.

Taken at face value, the story of Moses hitting the rock is pretty depressing. But read as a metaphor, it's actually quite beautiful in its encouragement to be gentle with ourselves. Perfectionism leads to violence. Maybe this story can help us learn, instead, to accept ourselves as we are: imperfect, dependent, ever changing.

I want to be gentle with myself and with my kid. I want to speak to the rock, not hit it. And when I mess up, as I inevitably will, I don't want to freak out. I want to take a breath, apologize, and try again. I want to tap my heart with love, rather than bang on it with anger. How else could we possibly get to the Promised Land?

33
Even the Holy Land Needs to Rest

If we allow ourselves to become totally overwhelmed
by our children's suffering, how can we be strong enough
to help them?

Once, driving Sylvia home from daycare, I suddenly heard a wail coming from the back seat. I looked at the rearview mirror to see her sunny face contorting with pain. "What's wrong, honey?" I asked, alarmed, and Sylvia sobbed, "No one wanted to play with me today!"

As an adult, I knew this was a normal thing to happen. But I knew that for Sylvia, it was truly painful. She felt like she'd been abandoned by her friends. And I felt a pain in my chest too. It may have been emotional rather than physical, but it *hurt*.

It's not just my own kid who can evoke this newfound extreme empathy in me. Ever since I became a mother, listening to the news regularly brings me to tears; I cry into the lasagna when I hear reports of people enduring terrible situations or—conversely—people bravely standing up for each other.

(I know that my own tears don't help those who are suffering; I do my best to transform them into action as well.)

This new sensitivity is a sort of superpower, a central part of the amazing spiritual journey of parenting. Indeed, spiritual traditions view our love for our children as a model for transcending the limits of the self. Buddhist teachings about compassion, for example, suggest trying to view everyone, even one's enemies, with a mother's love.

But this parental superpower has its dangers too. Even empathy needs its limits. After all, if we allow ourselves to become totally overwhelmed by our children's suffering—not to mention that of strangers—how can we be strong enough to help them?

And if we care for others' emotional or physical needs to the exclusion of our own, we'll eventually wear ourselves down to the point where we can't show up as parents, causing more suffering.

So where is the balance between empathy and boundaries, between caretaking and rest?

The book of Leviticus is full of rules, boundaries, and limits. Some of these are pretty hard for modern readers to relate to. Others, however, resonate with our contemporary experiences.

For instance, *shemitah*, which literally means "release," and refers to the laws surrounding letting the land of Israel rest in the seventh year. Moses instructs the people that after farming for six years, they must let the land of Israel lie fallow and restore itself every seventh year. It's a sort of Shabbat for the earth: six years of work and one year of rest.

If this commandment is observed—if the Israelites set boundaries on how much they work the land—the Torah's promised cycles of plenty will continue. But if they ignore it and farm straight through that seventh year, the land will grow desolate and will eventually be destroyed. In other words, limits are necessary for sustainability. This ancient Jewish prescription for environmental health, and the warning of consequences if boundaries are not observed, are terrifyingly relevant in the era of climate change.

And it contains a wider lesson, too, I think: that everyone needs rest, and boundaries, in order to care for our own emotional health and sustainability. Even parents.

Parenthood is demanding and challenging, and we're in it for the long haul. Can we apply the same care to our emotional lives that we are learning to show the earth and learn to parent more sustainably? Can we incorporate rest and self-nurturing into our own daily lives to avoid overfarming our own land, melting our own personal glaciers?

As a parent, I desperately hope that we as a species can figure out ways to heal the earth for our grandchildren and their grandchildren. And I also know that in my own life, I need to work toward sustainability, both physically and emotionally.

Because as parents of young children, we *are* the earth, source of shelter and food and love. We are where it all begins. We are home.

And as the Torah teaches us, even the Holy Land needs to rest.

34
The Möbius Strip of Life and Death

In Jewish tradition, this is what we do when someone dies: we bring food. It may not ease the mourners' pain, but it's a literal and symbolic manifestation of our love.

Parenting is full of paradoxes, the transcendent colliding with the everyday.

On the one hand, we parents experience up close and on a daily basis the miracle of existence, the intensity of love, the magic of oxytocin. On the other, we're constantly faced with the practical details that keep the whole thing going: an endless rotation of pouring cereal, wiping counters, folding laundry, and vacuuming floors.

The Torah, too, is an odd mix of sublime and mundane. Sometimes our holy texts dwell on the most heightened moments of human experiences: birth and death, exile and liberation. Other parts, however, focus on technicalities and specifics of everyday life. And these are sometimes interwoven in surprising and heartbreaking ways.

For example, two back-to-back chapters in Leviticus: in the first, we read a tragic story of a father's two sons' untimely death—and in the next, a highly detailed list of which foods are kosher and which aren't.

Here's the first story, about life and death and a strange, sacred, dangerous fire: Aaron is the brother of Moses and the first high priest of the Israelites. He has two adult sons, Nadav and Avihu, who also serve as priests in the Mishkan—until the terrible day when they offer a "strange fire" on the altar and are suddenly killed by God.

This is a mysterious story. Most commentators focus on that evocative offering, the "strange fire." Interpreters offer different theories about why the brothers' offering would cause their death. Some suggest that Nadav and Avihu were drunk, or that their sacrifice was offered in a spirit of rebelliousness or disrespect. Other commentators take the opposite approach, interpreting their deaths as a reward: Nadav and Avihu's offering was so holy that God gathered them up in a loving embrace of fire.

I've long been fascinated by this idea of the "strange fire." As with so many Torah stories, though, it reads differently to me as a mom. Now, when I read about Nadav and Avihu's death, I can't stop thinking about Aaron, their father. I imagine his shock and grief. I wonder how he handled his sons' sudden death at the hands of God.

The text doesn't really tell us. We see Moses turn to his grieving brother and say, "This is what Adonai meant by saying, 'Through those near to Me I show Myself holy, and gain glory before all the people.'" And we read Aaron's response: "And Aaron was silent" (Leviticus 10:3).

Moses's comment doesn't sound particularly sensitive to me; instead, it reads like one of those unhelpful platitudes people offer after the death of a beloved. So I'm glad the story gives Aaron a moment of silence for his private grief.

After this silence, though, the text moves on. And weirdly, it doesn't wait long—just sixteen verses—before diving into a list of rules about keeping kosher. God instructs Moses and Aaron together, teaching them which animals, bugs, fish, and birds the Israelites are allowed to eat and which they aren't.

On the surface, it's an odd juxtaposition, going from such a deep emotional episode to dietary protocols. But on a deeper level, it makes total sense to me.

After all, in Jewish tradition, this is what we do when someone dies: we bring food. It may not ease the mourners' pain, but it's a literal and symbolic manifestation of our love. Food is how we tether a mourning person to this world, and to our community, at a time when they are most vulnerable, closest to that line between life and death.

This is part of being alive: the highly emotional is interwoven with the utterly practical. It's a Möbius strip. On one side are the huge transformations: magic and terror, birth and death. Profound passages that explode our sense of time, restructure our lives, and change us forever.

On the other side: the small daily rules and rituals that structure our days. Eating and dressing and emailing and getting out the door and getting home and bath time and bed, and then starting all over again the next day.

These two halves are not separate at all, except in our minds.

We live our daily lives in the face of mystery: we are born, naked miracles, and at any moment we can return just as quickly to wherever we came from. Until that happens, there are meals to cook and dishes to wash and clothes to fold and walks to take and teeth to be brushed.

Sometimes we are the new mother, sometimes the mourner; sometimes we're the person bringing food. Over the course of life, we journey back and forth from side to side. From strange fire to making dinner, and back again.

35
Snuggling Is a Mini-Shabbat

Shabbat is not simply a set of laws to follow; it's an expression of a natural truth about rest, regeneration, and sustainability.

One of the best pieces of parenting advice I've ever gotten came from a stranger at a barbecue.

I was pregnant with our second child, Elijah—destined to be our in-house comedian, though we didn't know it yet. Meanwhile, two-year-old Sylvia was running around destroying the world, toddler-style.

It was July; I was enormous and extremely hot. As I watched my husband run interference between our charging daughter and a hot grill, I rubbed my belly and shook my head, wondering . . . how on earth would we handle a toddler *plus* an infant?

Just then, I heard a happy squeal and turned around to see a glimpse of my future as a mom of two. Her baby was crawling across the grass in a diaper, while her toddler studiously ripped apart a dandelion.

She noticed me looking at her, saw my belly and my toddler, and gave me that universal mother-of-young-kids smile that means, "I don't know you, but we're in this together."

That was all it took for me to ask this total stranger for advice. "How do you do it?" I blurted out, meaning, of course, "How am *I* going to do this?"

She gave me a warm, open smile. "Honestly," she said, "the best advice I got is something a friend told me before my second was born.

She said, when things get really, really bonkers, just drop every-thing, climb into bed with the kids, and snuggle. It's a lifesaver."

Drop everything and snuggle? That was the sum total of her parenting wisdom?

Over the years, though, I've realized that her seemingly simple advice resonates with a central, profound Jewish practice: Shabbat.

The word *Shabbat* comes from a root that means "to stop." It's related to the modern Hebrew word for "strike" (as in ceasing work), which makes sense; at its heart, a central part of Shabbat is doing exactly that.

In the Jewish worldview, Shabbat is not simply a set of laws to follow; it's an expression of a natural truth about rest, regen-eration, and sustainability. We rest every seventh day for the same reason the Torah prescribes letting the land lay fallow every seventh year—because living things need a break.

Once the sun goes down on Friday night, many observant Jews spend their time until sundown on Saturday focusing on food, rest, conversation, play, and spiritual practice. No work, no hustle, no planning, and, ideally, no stress. (That said, it's supposed to be a fun pause, not a solemn one; traditionally, sex is encouraged, at least between married couples!)

Anyway, when this wise mom counseled me to "drop every-thing and snuggle," it reminded me of this practice of Shabbat rest.

I think she was saying there's no built-in "Shabbat" when it comes to caring for our children. Our responsibility to them never ends. That's particularly true with the outrageous cost of childcare, at least in America; parents need more societal support. But no matter how much support we get, sometimes it's just going to be us and the kids.

So we need to be creative in carving out "mini-Shabbats"— moments of rest for ourselves and our kids, together.

I never saw that woman again, but I did find myself years later, in a moment of crisis, drawing on her advice. Aaron had to leave town for a family emergency; then, an ice storm shut down the entire city, leaving me alone with a two- and four-year-old in our one-bedroom apartment. We were there for days on end; we couldn't go for a walk because the sidewalks were too slippery, and even our local babysitter didn't feel safe driving to our house.

Desperate for a break, with none in sight for days, I stood there for a moment, feeling utterly overwhelmed as both kids fought on the floor beside me. Then I remembered that kind stranger's advice. I dropped everything, climbed in bed with the kids, and snuggled. And it worked.

It's just a part of parenting: those mutual meltdowns, sudden crises, extra-impossible moments when nothing is helping and everything is falling apart. When there's no one to take the kids for a minute and nowhere to go.

In these moments, it's time to call a strike. Not *from* our kids, but with them. To drop everything, hustle them in bed with us, and snuggle.

The rabbis say Shabbat is a taste of the world to come. This is one version of that future utopia. A big pause, a breath, a break: a moment when we hold close the ones we love and let everything else go.

36
Parenting in Dangerous Times

Together, we lead each other out of the darkness into the light of our full humanity.

In the early hours of the morning, I crawl into bed after showering the tear gas off my body. I know I am only one of many people who are also washing chemicals off their bodies, and the thought of our numbers comforts me.

All we did was to stand on public property with a crowd of peaceful protesters, holding signs that said Black Lives Matter. But we knew that at some point we were likely to face impact munitions and pepper spray, so we arrived in bike helmets and swim goggles and, if we had them, gas masks.

I crawl into bed beside my husband. In the morning I'll wake up and bring my kids to day camp.

My mind drifts back to a long-ago day in what feels like another lifetime. I was a new teacher, in my very early twenties, just beginning my second year at a small Jewish elementary school in Massachusetts. That morning our principal, Sandy, called us into the break room and told us somberly that the country seemed to be under attack. The World Trade Center had fallen, there were reports of planes still circling in the sky, and no one knew exactly how many there were or who was flying them.

Sandy made a decision: We would carry on teaching without telling the kids what was going on. With students as young as five in the building, we would let their families decide what to say.

Between classes, we teachers huddled around the radio listening for news, and when our ten-minute breaks were over, we wiped our tears and headed back into the classroom. All day we carried on: teaching the alphabet, multiplication tables, world history, Torah stories.

Since we were a Jewish school, we feared for the kids' safety in the face of potential antisemitic violence. The local police came to stand outside the front doors. In the classroom, I also thought of my students' emotional safety, and I knew it was more important than my grief in that moment. Looking back, I think that is the day I became a full adult.

On September 12, we returned to stand in front of our students again. This time they knew what had happened. We discussed what the attack on the World Trade Center meant for our country. We talked about what we knew and what we did not know. We acknowledged the fear of these times, and also modeled hope: not having all the answers, but also knowing what we believed in.

In recent years, in these complex, dangerous times, I've often thought back to that day. The details change over time, but the truth remains: we have to model hope. We can't know the outcome, but we can show our kids by example what it means to stand up for what we believe in—to have courage, faith, honesty, patience, and conviction. We can teach our kids about the kind of power that embraces vulnerability, that refuses to fall back on easy slogans, that refuses to hate.

One of my favorite Jewish teachings comes from *Pirkei Avot*: "In a place where there is no good person, strive to be a good person" (*Pirkei Avot* 2:5). (Full disclosure: the Hebrew word I'm translating as "good person" actually means "man"—but it's used here in the sense of mensch, a solid human being.)

When we look around us and see injustice, abuse of power, persecution, and discrimination, we have a choice: We can shake our heads and give up, or we can use our voices to express what we believe to be true.

We can teach our little ones ways to create a safe space in our own homes, demonstrate that our love for them is more powerful than our fear for the future, and show our older ones that we can and must act through our grief.

We who strive to be good people recognize that we who are called to be adults in the deepest sense cannot give into hate or hopelessness. We do not have that luxury. Instead, we must fight for what we know to be right and true. Not just for ourselves and our children and our sacred traditions, but for all those who are threatened.

Together, we lead each other out of the darkness into the light of our full humanity.

37
Parenting as *Tikun*

We can't fix everything broken in the world, but we can put one foot in front of the other.

My kids have their shy moments. But in general, they're both quicker to make friends than I ever was at their age (and already dressing themselves with a flair that I didn't develop until high school).

Still, like everyone, both of my kids sometimes feel excluded: birthday parties they're not invited to, bad days on the playground, outings where a best friend buddies up to another kid and ignores them.

It doesn't happen often, but each time, their pain brings me right back to the moments in my own life when I've felt excluded, and sometimes I have to bite my tongue to keep from crying with them.

The strength of this feeling always surprises me because this feeling—being shy, feeling excluded—wasn't the primary experience of my childhood. It was just a small thing that happened once in a while, an experience I suspect I share with every sensitive kid in this big and confusing world.

Still, that feeling is reawakened in parenting. And I'm starting to realize this is a basic truth of raising children: their new wounds awaken our old (sometimes very old) ones. It's one of the hardest things about being a parent, but also one of the most powerful, because reexperiencing this feeling can offer us profound opportunities for healing.

In Jewish tradition, this is called *tikun*, a Hebrew word that literally means "repair," but which encompasses many kinds of healing, mending, and repairing.

Tikun can be as deep as healing a childhood wound, or as simple as mending a tear in a favorite pair of pants; it can be as small as fixing a broken watch, or as large as working for justice for all humankind, as in the concept of *tikun olam*, literally "repairing the world."

One beautiful example of tikun in Jewish thought is connected to the very creation of the world. According to the parallel version of the creation story taught by the kabbalists, the world is a collection of broken shards, each containing a bit of divine light.

This mystical worldview tells us that every person, place, and object, however broken, contains its own spark of holiness. Divine energy courses through each of our experiences, even the most painful ones.

On a societal level, this means we all have the obligation to mend the world around us, in the form of tikun olam. Working toward repairing economic injustice, racial oppression, gender discrimination, and caring for the vulnerable is not a side project or a luxury, but a central mission—one of the most important things we can do during the short time we are alive.

And on a personal level, there is the inner healing we are each here to carry out. Each of us is a small world, say the medieval commentators. And as the Talmud explains, saving a single person is like saving the whole world. We are microcosms of all creation: like the world, we are broken, and like the world, we can heal.

When my midwife taught me about scar tissue massage after my second C-section, she didn't use the word tikun, but I think that's what she was talking about. Once the skin had healed, she said, I should gently massage the area with my fingers to break down the scar tissue. There were two levels of healing: first my skin would miraculously knit itself back together after being cut in two; then I could encourage that scar to release, allowing a deeper level of cellular healing to occur.

That tightness—the restricted, inflexible area of scar tissue—reminds me of what medieval Jewish mystics called a *k'lipah*, which means "a shell." Releasing a shell of emotional scar tissue lets our inner spark shine more brightly.

Which brings me back to the powerful mirror of parenting.

Coming face-to-face with our own brokenness, small or large, doesn't always feel good. But it's a gift, a necessary step in our healing. While our childhood pain remains deeply hidden, it's almost impossible to heal it. When we can see that pain, we can consider it as the adults we are now; we can integrate it, and perhaps even let it go.

As much as we try to protect our children, they, too, will have their wounds, in childhood and beyond. They, too, will need to heal. And they will need to help heal the world around them. It's part of what makes us able to grow and have compassion for each other's struggles. It's part of being human, baked into our design.

Tikun is a never-ending process. The best we can do is relax into it and remember that spark at the center of each broken shard. We won't be able to fix every messed-up thing that has been programmed into us; we can't fix everything broken in the world, but we can put one foot in front of the other and try to do our part.

Sometimes this means teaching our kids about social justice, or making ethical food and shopping choices for our families, or weighing where to send our kids to school.

Sometimes it means taking a deep breath and realizing that a wound has been touched, and that as uncomfortable as it is, this is not a disaster; it's an opportunity to begin to heal.

And sometimes it is as simple as showing up for our kids and ourselves. Snuggling, listening, holding their pain and our own.

In the end, that's love—the most powerful tikun there is.

38

My Toddler, My Teacher

I've had to grow less certain, more flexible. Less inclined to judge others, more inclined to realize I am in no position to judge.

This week, a friend came to visit, a former colleague from my teaching days. We haven't seen each other since before we had kids, but we seem to be on the same schedule: each of us with two kids the same ages.

We walked to the café down the street and sat outside at a picnic table, drinking iced coffee and talking about birth and motherhood. It turned out we had more in common than just the ages of our kids. We'd both expected our experience as teachers to help our parenting; instead, for both of us, that experience was actually making things harder in some ways.

Here's the thing: as teachers, we were used to running a tight ship. We planned our lessons in advance, we set clear expectations and (mostly) stuck to them, and—crucially—we said goodbye to our students at the end of each day.

As parents, a lot of that has gone out the window. Yes, clear expectations and consistency are still important. But there's a lot more winging it, and a lot less preparing in advance. And of course, the work doesn't end at 3:00 p.m.

Most importantly, we've both had to grow less certain, more flexible. Less inclined to judge others, more inclined to realize we are in no position to judge. And more aware—*so* aware—of all that lies beyond our control.

In other words, our kids are our teachers. And we teachers-turned-moms? We're here to learn.

Jewish tradition puts great emphasis on respecting our elders and honoring our parents, but there are also plenty of stories of elders learning from the younger generation.

For example, the words of Rabbi Chanina in the Talmud: "Much I have learned from my teachers, more from my colleagues, and most of all from my students." For a culture that reveres learning and values teachers so highly, this is a beautiful teaching about the power of the younger generation to school *us*.

Another example I love comes from the Torah itself. It's a somewhat obscure story about the five daughters of Zelophehad (not high on the Hebrew-baby-name lists, I'm sorry to report). When their father dies leaving no sons, these women are left without land. According to the laws of inheritance Moses has taught, women aren't allowed to inherit property.

But Zelophehad's daughters take matters into their own hands. They argue before Moses that women should be able to inherit property, at least in this specific case.

Moses, with his trademark humility, admits he isn't sure what to do and turns to God. God agrees with the sisters: their father's land belongs to them. And just like that, a new precedent for women's inheritance is set.

As a feminist, I've loved this story for years. Granted, it's only a limited precedent for women's inheritance, dependent on a lack of brothers and requiring the women to marry within their tribe. But it's still a pretty great start for the ancient world.

But these days, I'm also appreciating this story in a whole new way: as a mother.

After all those years in a quasi-parental role, leading the Israelites through the desert, Moses still has a lot to learn from the younger generation. No matter how wise he is, they can see things he can't. And he doesn't seem embarrassed by this fact; not at all. Instead, he seems to gracefully accept the fact that part of his job is to teach the children of Israel—and another part of his job is to learn from them.

My kids aren't yet ready to present me with legal arguments, though their negotiation skills have begun giving me a run for my money. But already, they are my teachers.

Humility, love, patience, perspective, humor. My kids have whole new lessons planned for me every day, without even needing to prepare.

PART 4

Parenting as Spiritual Practice

God, the Imperfect Parent

39

What Jewish Mysticism Can Teach Us about Parenting (and Which Shoe to Put on First Every Morning)

Our kids have a way of humbling us and bringing us down to earth in a split second if we get too esoteric.

S ometimes, when I lean over to kiss one of my children's foreheads as I tuck them into bed, I suddenly feel the echo of all our ancestors kissing *their* kids goodnight, going back in time. For a moment I'm released from the mundane practical details of my life. I'm not just *me*; I'm larger than that, connected with something timeless and transcendent.

And then the next morning we're back to the hustle of fitting small arms into small T-shirts to get out the door in time for daycare.

We all live in this balance of practical and transcendent, and Judaism reflects that dichotomy.

On one hand, our tradition is full of practical rules and laws. Which foods are kosher; what prayers to say when; how to take care of those who need help; how to mourn, how to celebrate.

The rabbis even suggest that we put the right shoe on first in the morning, rather than the left (more on this later).

And then, to balance out these practical directives, there's the transcendent realm of Jewish mysticism. By definition, mysticism is hard to label. *Merriam-Webster* says it's "a theory postulating the possibility of direct and intuitive acquisition of ineffable knowledge or power." Personally, I think mysticism boils down to this: life is essentially a mystery, but that doesn't mean we can't try to understand it.

Jewish mysticism, or kabbalah, covers a wide range of thought: visions of heavenly angels and demons, subtle energy maps of the human body, and thousands of breathing and meditation techniques for connecting with the Divine. Traditionally, the study of mysticism was considered too dangerous for general consumption. It was reserved for a limited group: men over forty, deeply learned in Torah, married, with children.

This old restriction is obviously sexist, and I'm glad it's no longer maintained in most modern communities. But I *do* love that last restriction—that before delving into the mysteries, we must become parents.

This acknowledges parenthood as a transformation, one that can ground us in preparation for the mystical heights and depths of kabbalah. Too much mystical study can be dangerous; there are stories in our tradition about times when it pulled a person's head so far into the clouds that their feet left the ground entirely. Having children protects us from this. Our kids tie us to this world, and they have a way of humbling us and bringing us down to earth in a split second if we get too esoteric.

Mysticism can support us in our parenting too. One of my favorite mystical Jewish concepts, which I draw on every single day, is the idea of balancing compassion with boundaries.

The basic concept is that two massive forces balance each other —both in the Divine and, since we are made in the image of

God, in each of us. On the right side is compassion—in Hebrew, *chesed*. This represents loving-kindness, openness, forgiveness, unconditional love—in a word, "Yes." On the left side, balancing it out, is the concept of boundaries—represented by the Hebrew word *gevurah*, meaning "might" or "valor." Limits, rules, structure, and consequences—in a word, "No."

We instinctively think of "yes" as kinder than "no," but the truth is that they are both equally necessary.

A baby can't be born without both of these forces. Chesed is the womb, nourishing and safe. Gevurah is labor, a sometimes painful, powerful, and necessary push into the light.

As infants grow into toddlers, we parents continue this constant dance between compassion and boundaries. We love our children with the earth-shattering, self-obliterating love of chesed. And yet part of our job is also to set limits, to use gevurah. We have to teach them not to run into traffic, not to bite their playmates, and not to smear applesauce on the wall. If we don't give them this structure, we aren't doing our jobs as parents.

The balance between unconditional love and boundaries is constantly shifting. Sometimes our kids have a rough day and need a little extra love and patience. Sometimes they push the boundaries to a point that requires more firmness than usual. There's no single answer; we just have to keep on rebalancing, day after day, using our hearts as a gauge to keep us grounded in the center.

And an even more difficult part of our job is also to balance compassion and judgment toward ourselves and our parenting.

The judgment part is easy, at least for me. I feel absolutely awful when I yell at one of my kids for some small infraction, see them burst into tears, and realize I've brought out the big guns for no good reason. Or lose my temper not because of their behavior but because of my own exhaustion or stress.

It's so tempting, in those moments, to be angry with myself, to slam down on the side of gevurah and judge myself as a bad parent. But even then, compassion needs to be part of the equation —toward ourselves, as much as our kids.

Remember how the rabbis advise putting on our right shoe first in the morning? That's their way of saying, "Lean toward chesed"—the right side, in kabbalistic thinking. Mysticism sees the physical world as an expression of deeper truths, energies, and realities. When we put on our right shoe, we are saying, *I love you, world. I'll do my best to keep the balance between compassion and boundaries today, but it won't be fifty-fifty; I'll lean ever so slightly toward compassion.*

And then we tie our shoes and step out into the utterly mundane, utterly transcendent world.

40

My Kids Bring Out the Best and Worst in Me

Maybe God's behavior toward the children of Israel is just what it sounds like: a hot mess. And maybe that's exactly why we need to read Torah stories.

Sometimes, I love seeing myself as a mother. Taking care of my kids, I can feel how my heart has opened and grown strong through parenthood. I can feel the tremendous power of love passing through me; I watch myself stretch to meet my kids' needs, and I think with pride, "I couldn't have done *that* a year ago!"

But that's only half the story.

For me, being a mother is also the spiritual equivalent of looking into one of those magnifying mirrors that point out every pore and flaw. Yes, I can see the depth of my own capacity for love, my strength in how I show up for my kids; but at the same time, every day I'm also forced to witness myself in unflattering light, with my rough edges made even rougher. Not how I'd like to be, necessarily, but how I am.

Is this a pleasant experience? Not particularly. But it also happens to be great preparation for the holiest time in the Jewish year: the ten Days of Awe, a period that begins with Rosh Hashanah and ends with Yom Kippur.

During this time, we examine ourselves and take stock of who we are on the deepest level. We consider our failings of the past year, the ways we could have been better, the parts of ourselves we don't like to see.

Pre-kids, I would do a lot of journaling during this season to help me see my own flaws more clearly and identify what I wanted to change. Now, it's easier. I see myself at my worst regularly. When my kid dumps a full bowl of penne with sauce on the floor (and to think I secretly puréed zucchini into that sauce to try and get some vitamins in her!). When she tries to climb on top of her baby brother to reach the silverware drawer. When I let a two-year-old provoke my inner fury.

I can feel especially shaken by the rage that sometimes rises in me. So I'm relieved to find in the Torah that I'm not alone—not just that other mothers experience this, as I know they do, but that God, too, seems to have some mom-rage as part of "parenting" the children of Israel.

Toward the end of the Torah, Moses recites a long poem to the children of Israel. He's preparing to die, so this is an important speech. Yes, he talks about how much God loves them, but he also tells them how ticked off God is about their transgressions.

Moses describes God's rage against their idolatry and ingratitude, and how God has threatened to punish them with famine, plague, and "fanged beasts." Finally, in the end, Moses describes how God calms down and decides to bless them after all.

Why would the Torah describe God this way, like an exasperated parent who can't take it anymore? I'd expect a deity to be above this sort of response—to model, instead, the perfect parenting we're taught in how-to books. Firm but infinitely loving, doling out consequences instead of punishments, and always above the temptation to let mere toddlers (or, in this case, mere humans) provoke an emotional reaction with their actions.

To be fair, the Torah was written over three thousand years ago in the ancient Near East, and they had some very different ideas about parenting in those days. "Spare the rod, spoil the child" comes directly from the book of Proverbs (13:24). So I guess it's possible that the ancient world had no problem with an angry parent; maybe God actually *is* modeling good parenting by the standards of the time.

But as a mother, I have another theory. Maybe God's behavior toward the children of Israel is just what it sounds like: a hot mess. And maybe that's exactly why we need to read these stories.

After all, by the end of Moses's speech, God has recovered from that terrible anger and returned to a place of compassion. God lost control for a moment and then regained it—something that happens dozens of times in the course of a day spent parenting young children.

If this happens to the Omnipotent, who are *we* to think it won't happen to us?

Perhaps after witnessing God's mistakes, we can be more compassionate about our own epic parenting fails.

The Days of Awe are the perfect moment to work on this compassion—forgiving not just others, but also ourselves. But this sacred period comes only once a year, and that's not enough. So it's a good thing that, according to our tradition, the opportunity for repair is always available to us.

The rabbis call this repair "teshuvah"; it's usually translated as "repentance" but literally means something like "returning," in the sense that apologizing returns us to our best selves. *Teshuvah* is a main focus of Yom Kippur, but it's not limited to that sacred day. We can ask forgiveness for our mistakes and return to our best selves anytime. It's within reach every day, as many times a day as we need it. It's infinite.

It's not a coincidence that we are at our best and our worst when we're with our kids. Whatever in us needs to grow—to be pushed, stretched, smoothed, or strengthened—our kids will show us that place, in the magnifying mirror of motherhood (or, more generally, parenthood).

In this way, our kids are our teachers. And we have to be patient with ourselves, because sometimes it takes a while to learn—especially when you're an adult.

41
Fleeting Blessings

Three simple lines from the Torah have been a conduit
of blessings for millennia.

Three decades after my bat mitzvah, I can still remember the
tingly feeling of holiness that passed over me when the rabbi
put his hands on my shoulders, smiled at me with twinkly eyes,
and chanted the Hebrew priestly blessing in his deep, resonant
voice.

While Rabbi Saltzman sang, a pipe organ played minor
chords, and a choir in robes sang solemnly. (I didn't realize until
later how much of the aesthetics of my huge Reform congregation
were borrowed from Christianity.) Still, though the pipe organ was
a modern twist, the blessing was ancient. The Temple priests, two
thousand years ago, spoke these same words when they blessed
the assembled Israelites in Jerusalem:

May God bless you and keep you.

May God shine God's face on you and give you grace.

May God give favor to you and grant you peace.
(Numbers 6:24–26)

Now I bless my own b'nei mitzvah students with these words
during their ceremonies, and that same feeling of sacred energy
travels through my body.

I find it magical that these three simple lines have been a
conduit of blessing for millennia. They're beautiful in themselves,
and I think their syllables have grown even more powerful from
all those generations of mouths reciting them, of love directed
through them.

Rabbis and other Jewish leaders aren't the only ones to use these ancient sacred blessings regularly. Every Friday night, as Shabbat begins, like so many Jewish parents around the world, I use the same words to bless my children.

I think this tradition comes from the fact that we parents (no matter how religious or not-religious we are) have a lot in common with ancient priests and modern rabbis. We are responsible for taking care of our little ones, and for teaching them how to live, and for teaching them our traditions so they can carry them on after us. Like ancient priests, like modern rabbis, we are a conduit for blessings.

Different families have different traditions around blessing the children on Friday night. In our family, right after lighting Shabbat candles, I place both my hands gently on Sylvia's head. I lean in, whisper the blessing into her curls, and kiss her. As if it weren't already the sweetest moment of my week, recently she's taken to saying "I bless Papa too?" and whispering gibberish against his forehead. And then I bless Elijah (who's usually in my arms) and kiss his forehead, as he stares up at me with his big blue eyes.

I use the traditional Hebrew words, but English works too, or—like Sylvia—you can make up your own blessing. For you theater kids, there's even a full-on musical version: *Fiddler on the Roof*'s "Sabbath Prayer" song.

Recently I met friends for a drink—two moms, a couple whose kids are way older than mine. They talked about getting ready to send their youngest kid off to college, and hearing their excitement, and their considerable sadness, jolted me awake.

In the rush and challenge of early parenthood, it's so easy to forget that one day my kids will be fully grown people who go on dates, choose majors, and are legally responsible for their own actions. I found myself experiencing the oddest longing to run home to my kids' bedroom, place my hands gently on their sleeping heads, and bless them.

I was grateful to be reminded that our time together in this particular family constellation—young kids scampering around the house—is limited. The ritual of blessing my kids is such a beautiful way to appreciate this version of our family, exactly as we all are in this moment, which will be gone before I know it.

It's magic, really: how these three-thousand-year-old words are perfect for marking this very moment. Whispering them, I have a momentary break from the chaos of early parenthood. Blessing my children, I appreciate my own fleeting blessings.

42
It's Okay Not to Love Every Stage

The single word *parenthood* fails to convey the ever-changing nature of the work.

Some people are just not baby people. Maybe it's the spit-up, or the crying, or the whole preverbal thing. For whatever reason, babies just don't do it for them.

Me? I love them. Mine, other people's—doesn't matter as long as they're babies.

I love how they lie against my chest like a little snuggly package of human warmth and potential. I love their weight in my arms and how perfectly they fit on my lap. I love their squishy little faces and their weird giant eyes.

My challenge comes later in the game: when it's toddler time.

Around the time Sylvia turned one, it was like a switch flipped—suddenly she was entirely mobile without any sense of her own limits, like a self-driving car gone berserk.

A couple of weeks earlier, I'd been able to sit peacefully on a blanket with a fellow mom as long as I kept one eye on my crawling babe. Now, any attempt at social time ended abruptly. "Sorry," I'd say mid-sentence, then bound off to prevent my wobbly-but-walking child from eating bark chips, torturing the host's cat, licking the play structure, or toddling across the street and escaping forever.

"I'm not really a toddler person" was easy to say when I didn't have a toddler. But when my own kid reached that stage, it sounded sort of messed up. I felt guilty: how could I love my kid so much and enjoy our day-to-day interactions so little? There were plenty of cute moments, of course, but in general, when I was honest with myself, I found this stage exhausting and boring.

To make matters worse, Sylvia was adorable. Well-meaning strangers were constantly passing us in the grocery store, smiling at her pigtails, and saying conspiratorially to me, "Such a cute age." Was I missing the best part of being a parent?

Then an angel appeared in the grocery store, in the form of a total stranger.

The scene: Sylvia was having a meltdown in the bread aisle. I was deep breathing. A woman was approaching with her shopping cart. As she maneuvered past our drama, she gave me a wry smile and said, "Survive 'til five." Then she deftly wheeled around my child's splayed form on the floor and disappeared around the corner.

I froze right there by the hot dog buns. It was okay to sort of hate this stage? It was okay to just . . . survive?

In that moment, I felt permission. Permission to have my experience without judging it. Permission to be bored and annoyed. Permission to love my kid, while not loving this developmental stage. Permission to just get through it, rather than having to enjoy it. I smiled all the way through checkout.

Later I found out that this understanding—that children enter a different stage around age five or six—is also echoed in the Talmud, when the great sage Rav suggests that six is the age at which students should begin coming to school. Apparently they didn't want tantrums in the study hall either. I get it!

This Talmudic teaching reflects a core truth: the single, simple word *parenthood* can't convey the ever-changing nature of the work. Parenting a baby, who wants to nurse and sleep and be bounced up and down, is totally different from parenting a preteen who's begging for a phone—or, if you're reading this in the future, whatever magical electronic gadget is the current equivalent of a phone.

And then when they're teens, oy vey, I don't even want to think about what that will entail.

And the changes happen so *fast*: a warp-speed superhero movie where they seem to shed their old selves as easily as a snake sheds its skin. "What do you *mean* you don't like pizza?" I demand as Elijah, my dedicated pizza lover, makes a face and pushes dinner away. He shrugs; yesterday, pizza was his favorite, and today it's not.

And as they change, what they need from us changes. One day we're obsessing over feeding and burping techniques; the next, we're trying to teach basic bicycling skills and conflict resolution. The ongoing work of parenting is really a series of vastly different jobs. Seen this way—*of course* my enjoyment of parenting fluctuates wildly with my kids' ages.

I'm grateful to that angel in the grocery store for teaching me that loving my kids is totally separate from loving the stage they happen to be in at the moment. That it's okay to have favorite ages and stages.

After all, we don't hold it against teachers if they prefer working with cuddly preschoolers, or if they're especially passionate about teaching college-level philosophy. Some doctors decide to specialize in pediatrics; others are drawn to geriatrics. Society has room for all of us; in fact, it *needs* all of us, with our particular likes and dislikes, our skills and our interests.

Together, we all add up to a society that can provide love, attention, education, and care at every stage of our lives.

Our time here on earth is brief, and childhood is far briefer. And day-to-day parenting is a balancing act: holding fast to our love for our kids, while keeping a loose hold on the current version of them, so we can let them morph into their next iteration.

Our kids are always disappearing before our eyes, always turning into the next version of themselves. And so are we—it's just a little less obvious. That's the nature of things. Sometimes bitter, sometimes sweet. And whatever stage we're in, it won't last forever.

43

Falling in Order to Rise

I want my kids to read these Torah stories and know that it's okay not to be perfect.

Have you seen that soap opera about the dysfunctional family where, just before a big wedding, the father tricks his daughter's fiancé into marrying her sister? And then the son-in-law ends up marrying *both* daughters, who are soon competing to see who can have the most babies? And then finally the guy takes off with both sisters in the middle of the night, taking the grandkids, running away from the father while stealing his most precious possession?

Just kidding, it's not a soap opera—it's the book of Genesis.

The father is Laban, the son-in-law is Jacob, and those two sisters with their incredibly complicated relationship and shared husband are Rachel and Leah.

Now that I'm a parent, I treasure these stories about super-complicated families. I appreciate how up-front our tradition is about the difficulties of living together, even when we love each other; the ways in which we fail each other, then dig deep and apologize and try harder, then fail again, but never stop loving one another.

It's fluid, a never-ending sine wave that goes up and down, carrying us into the future.

This wave image resonates with one of my favorite Chasidic concepts: *yeridah l'shem aliyah*, which means "falling in order to rise." According to this idea, challenges are not only inevitable but necessary to our growth. In order to learn, we need to mess up; only when we have fallen can we rise.

I thought of this concept when I read poet Diane di Prima's account of losing her mother as an adult in her book *Memoirs of a Beatnik*. Her mother had tried to hide the ups and downs of life, keeping her home determinedly cheerful and positive, and so her children had learned to keep their struggles to themselves.

Di Prima describes how, after their mother's funeral, she and her siblings speak with each other openly, as they never have before:

> The day of Emma's funeral I returned with my two brothers to my brother Frank's house in New Jersey, and the three of us talked for the first time in our lives of some of the darker stuff. It was as if a vast weight had lifted. We learned, for one thing, that each of us thought himself / herself the black sheep of the family—the major disappointment in Emma's life. We exchanged information that we'd each kept secret: a pending divorce, a chronic illness in one of our children. Information we'd kept to ourselves to avoid breaching the cheerfulness, the determined perfection of our lives.

Reading about these adult siblings finally admitting the imperfect reality of their lives, I can feel their hearts opening to each other. Yeridah l'shem aliyah: we can't rise together unless we are honest about our failings. Sharing our deepest struggles allows us to love each other in ways that are impossible otherwise.

Di Prima's story helps me understand why I am so drawn to the story of Jacob, Rachel, and Leah. It's not just the drama— it's the honesty. Our ancestors aren't perfect people doing perfect things, but highly complicated people with openly messy family lives. Perhaps this is why, despite their many betrayals of each other, I feel so much love between Rachel and Leah and Jacob.

It's that complicated kind of family love, mixed up with what di Prima calls "the darker stuff," the kind we can only reach when we stop pretending to be perfect. A sacred sort of deep connection we can only earn over time, through mistakes, forgiveness, and more mistakes.

Each fall, we celebrate the festival of Simchat Torah, when we complete the annual Torah reading cycle and begin all over again. This process happens over and over in our lives, just as we read these Torah stories over and over, year after year.

Simchat Torah literally means "the joy of Torah," and—as the name suggests—this holiday is a big party, with the Torah at the center. We take the scrolls out of the Ark; we sing and dance with them, holding them as if they were babies. In my own synagogue, the children sit cross-legged in the center of the sanctuary while the adults unroll the entire Torah scroll, forming a giant circle that surrounds and protects our kids, letting them see every letter of their sacred stories.

Looking at the children of my community encircled by their ancient stories, I think how lucky we are to have these legends. They've been passed down by so many generations, and now they are ours to savor, to examine, to argue against, and to pass down to our own kids. All those beautiful, dysfunctional ancestors, fumbling their way through relationships and spirituality, learning as they go, just like us.

I want my kids to read these stories and know that it's okay not to be perfect. They will mess up, and so will I and every single person on this earth.

Each year, each month, each week, we do the best we can. We try to show up for each other; sometimes we succeed, sometimes we fail. We mess up and try to do better next time. And then we rewind the scroll all the way back to the beginning and start again.

That's what it means to be human. We fall in order to rise: this is how we learn about love.

44

We All Add Up to the Perfect Parent

Together we try to build a society in which everyone is connected, cared for, and able to offer their gifts.

I recently went on a walk with a friend who's making some changes in her life.

She'd always planned on being a stay-at-home mom, but to her own surprise, after eighteen months at home with her kid, she's starting to look for daycare.

Having gone through a similar change myself, I was curious about her thought process. "What changed?" I asked, as we headed into the park near her house.

"Before I had kids," she answered, "I thought—why even *have* a baby if you're just going to hand it to someone else to raise it all day long? And now I'm like, oh yeah, I get it. My kid needs to do his thing, and I need to do my thing, and then we're both happy to see each other in the afternoon."

As she spoke, I remembered something I'd seen posted on a neighborhood mom group: a request for advice, written by a mom in deep distress.

This mom was a lawyer, and, unlike my friend, she'd returned to work after maternity leave, leaving her kid with a full-time nanny—a plan that had seemed totally reasonable, pre-baby. But now she was miserable. She cried every day when she kissed her kid goodbye, and cried all the way to work on her forty-five-minute commute. "I feel like I'm missing out on the most important thing in life," she wrote, "being with my baby."

I don't know what that mom decided to do, but I read her story around the time that I was coming to realize that my own plan wasn't working either—though in the opposite direction. I'd planned to stay at home with my baby; it turned out I desperately needed to work in order to be happy. Reading her words helped me realize that I wasn't alone. Sometimes our instincts for our future selves are right; other times, we can't know what we need until we need it.

It took me a while to realize (or to admit to myself) that I'd been wrong about what I wanted. I only wish I'd done it sooner. When we finally found full-time care for Sylvia at an in-home day-care in our neighborhood, my happiness level rose palpably. The couple who ran the daycare were a pair of sweet, loving Deadheads with three kids of their own and a giant white dog. Sylvia loved going there. She loved the dog, the play kitchen, the other kids, the bin full of tutus, and the snacks.

I was conscious, as I dropped Sylvia off each morning, of the overlapping layers of labor, of care, of the interweaving of family and community.

My neighbors' work, caring for children, is crucial. So is the work of stay-at-home parents. So is the work done by nannies, grandparents who help out, parents and guardians who send their kids to daycare, and early-childhood educators and elementary school teachers, waiting right around the corner, many of whom have kids and grandkids themselves. Together, we all add up to a functioning society.

The Torah has a model for this collaborative society weaving. In the desert, the Israelites are told to assemble a beautiful structure, a traveling prayer tent called the Mishkan. Each person is asked to bring what they are best able to contribute, and together they create a structure that is bigger than any one person.

The people bring aromatic spices, essential oils, handwoven cloth of deep purple and blue, and fine woodwork, and they donate jewelry that is melted down to make lamps and bowls.

The result must have been gorgeous, and I bet it smelled good too. It's an oasis of art, collaboration, and refuge for the road-weary Israelites. They're still wandering, but they now have a sacred tent that travels with them.

There's a bigger purpose to all this beauty too. The Mishkan will be the Israelites' first taste of home, a place to worship God in the unforgiving desert. And they are learning to work together too; it's the ultimate DIY community project, every single piece contributed by a group of formerly enslaved people learning to be free.

In the society they are building, everyone will have something to contribute. Some excel in the ability to care for young children. Others have a talent for weaving cloth, carving wood, or working with metal. Or work in government, or retail, or art, or service, or medicine.

I've been trying to avoid saying "It takes a village," but really, that's what I'm saying. No one person can do it all, not even the most heroic stay-at-home parent. We are all part of a larger system. Together, we try to build a society in which everyone is connected, cared for, and able to offer their gifts. Whether that gift is staying home with our own child, caring for someone else's, or doing some other sacred work.

Together, it all adds up to a modern Mishkan. Together, we all add up to the perfect parent.

45
Love and Rules

These are the rules, the simple work of love.

W hen God gives Moses the Torah on Mount Sinai, there's a lot of pomp and circumstance. So much so, in fact, that traditional commentators often compare this moment to a wedding.

As a former wedding musician, I've seen more than my share of fancy celebrations, and I concur—the description in the book of Exodus does read like a big-ticket wedding. There's the dramatic natural setting, the careful preparation, and at the center, the vows—in this case, the Ten Commandments, eternally binding the Israelites to God.

There's even thunder and lightning, God's version of an elaborate sound and light show.

After such a blowout, you might expect an equally amazing honeymoon. Instead, the Torah launches into a highly unromantic list of rules and laws. Some representative examples: What to do if someone asks you to watch their cow, and the cow dies. What sort of food priests are allowed to eat. How they shouldn't build stairs to ascend to the altar so that (wearing robes) they don't accidentally flash the people as they perform sacrifices. Not exactly the stuff of romance.

All these practical rules feel out of place as a follow-up to a wedding—but not all commentators interpret this moment in Israelite history as a wedding. Another perspective connects the moment of Revelation in the Torah to a very different life-cycle moment: toddlerhood.

If we interpret the Exodus from Egypt as a birth narrative, this would make the Israelites (metaphorically) newborns as they begin their wanderings in the desert. In this framework, when they arrive at Mount Sinai, they are basically toddlers. And considering the Israelites as toddlers instead of newlyweds, these unromantic rules make a lot more sense.

Any parent of a toddler knows that as the miracle of birth recedes, the work grows more complicated. Parenting an infant is pretty much about keeping it alive; parenting a toddler means an unending litany of small, everyday rules.

Don't climb on the table! Don't grab your friend's toy! Don't pull mama's hair! Don't run into the street, draw on the wall with crayons, dump your water glass out on the floor, put your hands in the toilet bowl, throw your toy record player at your brother, eat Papa's earplugs, or run around the house with a toothbrush in your mouth. Please.

Please?

The Israelites, like toddlers, are growing, step by step, into full peoplehood. And in order to do this, they need guidance. Specific guidance, point by point, to carry them from helplessness to resilience. It's not romantic, but it's crucial.

Raising toddlers is all about this unromantic, crucial work. It's about gently teaching limits and boundaries, over and over; it's about showing up, day after day. This is the holy work of being present, the holy work of love. Come to think of it, in some ways, it's not so different from the years that follow a marriage (if we're lucky).

Rabbi Lord Jonathan Sacks, for many years the chief rabbi of the United Kingdom, commented on this moment in the Torah. These laws, Rabbi Sacks writes in *Covenant & Conversation*, "sometimes seem an anticlimax after the breathtaking grandeur of the Revelation at Sinai . . . but without the details, the vision floats in heaven. With them the Divine Presence is brought down to earth, where we need it most."

Creating a new human is, like the Exodus from Egypt, a miracle of the highest order. But, as Rabbi Sacks says, miracles are just the beginning. The Divine Presence resides most power-fully in the details.

I teach Sylvia to look both ways before we cross the street. I hold her hand until we reach the sidewalk, even when she tries to pull away. When it's safe, I let her run as fast as she can.

These are the rules, the simple work of love.

46

What Exactly Do We Owe Our Kids?

It would be nice if there were some kind of checklist:
if you've done these things, you're officially a good parent.

How do I mess up as a mom? Let me count the ways.

The times I yell when I should hug, or scroll when I should listen, or scold when I should ask . . . actually, that's too depressing. I'm not going to count the ways.

At least I know I'm not alone in this. If I've learned one thing as a mom, it's that (I'm pretty sure) messing up is a basic part of the job description.

Still, occasionally I can't help but wonder: on a basic level, am I doing well *enough*? It would be nice if there were some kind of . . . checklist. If you've done these things, you're officially a good parent. Congratulations! Stop worrying about it!

Unfortunately, the Torah doesn't offer us a checklist. Instead, it's full of stories about highly questionable parenting: Noah gets drunk and exposes himself to his adult sons. Abraham takes Isaac up a mountain and almost sacrifices him. Intruders threaten Lot, and he says they can take his daughters as long as they'll spare his city. Oy.

Some of the Torah's parenting stories, like that last one, are totally atrocious. Others convey a lot of love along with the trauma. Yet a surprising number of them contain some spectacularly bad decisions.

In a way, it's reassuring that Torah sets the parenting bar so very low. Still, on a practical level, it's not very helpful in terms of advice.

Perhaps this is why, many centuries later, the rabbis compiling the Talmud decided a parenting checklist might actually be a good idea after all. Or maybe they just realized that parents could use a little guidance. Whatever the reason, here's their checklist. According to those rabbis, at a minimum, a parent is obligated to . . .

Circumcise male children

Redeem firstborn sons through the ritual of *pidyon haben*

Teach them Torah

Marry them off

Teach them a trade

(Some also add teaching them to swim, which makes sense to me.)

Since these rules were written two thousand years ago, not all of them translate for modern readers. For instance, the original text talks only about boys; from its heterocentric perspective, it commands us "to marry them off to a woman." This leaves queer people and women out of the story; not very helpful.

So—here's (one version of) a modern checklist of what we need to do as parents, drawing on the Talmud's ideas in more contemporary language:

Teach our kids that they are Jewish

Remember that they are not really "ours"—we all belong to something bigger

Pass our traditions down

Accept our children's gender identity and sexuality

Teach them to care for themselves, as they are able

And yeah, swimming lessons are a good idea too

Following the rabbinic tradition of looking for meanings beneath the precise details, I might further shorten this checklist to four main goals:

Loving our children

Keeping them safe

Passing down our traditions

Teaching them to need us less

These rules seem simple enough on a quick read. But look a little closer, and it turns out they contain opposing impulses. We're obligated to keep our little kids from drowning, but we also have to teach them to swim. We have to feed them and also teach them how to feed themselves. We have to love them as their unique selves and also teach them they come from a tradition that is larger than any single person. We have to hold them tight, and when it's time, we have to let them go.

These days, when I find myself wondering if I'm doing okay as a mom, I try to remember that checklist. Even in the moments when I mess up—when I catch myself staring at my phone while my kid tugs on my leg, or at the end of a long day where I've yelled way more than I meant to—I'm determined to stop imagining their adult selves processing my shortcomings in therapy. Making myself miserable doesn't help anyone.

Instead, I give them a hug. I tell them I love them. And then I look up the deadline for swim-lesson signup.

Parenting is infinite; we are literally never done. But sometimes we owe ourselves the relief of knowing "I did it today." Maybe not every minute, maybe not perfectly—but we did it. And tomorrow, we'll wake up and do it again.

47
Mantras for the Marathon of Motherhood

As with marathons, simply showing up, step after step, means you're winning. And sometimes mantras help you get through.

A few years ago, I ran the Portland Marathon. To be more specific, I very slowly jogged the marathon, taking multiple stretch breaks, while volunteers along the way asked me, with concerned looks, "Are you okay?"

It took almost six hours, but yes, I was okay, every step of the way. Despite the disgusting blister on my foot, the searing line of fire that ran down my hamstring, and the fact that many of my fellow marathoners had finished hours earlier, I kept whispering under my breath, "You are strong. You are powerful." And saying those words made them come true.

I'd learned this mantra technique through a podcast about marathon training. I trained alone, so this podcast was my only companion across the long miles, and I listened to it obsessively. I'd never really thought of myself as a mantra person, but the podcasters were basically my coaches. So when they talked about the power of positive self-talk, I decided to overlook my initial resistance and give it a shot.

At first I felt self-conscious about whispering, "I am strong, I am powerful," as I slowly made my way north on Willamette

Boulevard. But the longer the training runs grew, the less I thought about it. Over and over I chanted it, red-faced, timing my footsteps with the phrases: "I am strong. I am powerful." Struggling up the steep slope at the foot of the St. Johns Bridge, I borrowed another line from the podcast: "I eat hills for breakfast."

I'd originally dismissed mantras as cheesy, but to my surprise, I found that they totally worked. No matter how aspirational the words felt when I started a run, after a hundred repetitions, I started to believe them. "I am strong. I am powerful. I eat hills for breakfast."

On marathon day, my eyes filled with tears when I saw my kids and Aaron cheering me on at the finish line. "You have a medal, Mama!" Elijah exclaimed, handing me a bouquet of hydrangeas. "Did you *win*?!"

"Well . . . " I said, giving him a sweaty hug, "actually, I was pretty close to last. But everyone who finishes a marathon gets a medal. It's so hard to do, just *finishing* is sort of like winning." The kids were skeptical, but I knew it was true.

I'm not the first to compare parenting to marathon running: a long slog, with exhilarating highs and excruciating lows. As with marathons, simply showing up, step after step, means you're winning. And sometimes mantras help you get through.

While I ran up and down the bridges of Portland chanting about eating hills for breakfast, I thought about the great Chasidic rabbi, Nachman of Breslov (1772–1810). His teachings, too, often focus on getting through difficult moments.

Rebbe Nachman famously struggled with extreme highs and lows, experiencing soaring visions and deep despair. Reading his words and knowing a little about his suffering, I get the sense that he was running his own spiritual marathon—surrounded by thousands of followers, but ultimately alone.

Perhaps this is why one of the most famous of his teachings offers its own kind of spiritual pep talk. Known as "Azamra," this chapter from the classic collection of his teachings, *Likutey Moharan*, offers a vision of radical love for others and for ourselves: "Know that you must judge all people favorably. This applies even to the worst of people. You must search until you find some little bit of good in them . . . . If you can just find this little bit of good and judge them favorably, you can truly elevate them."

Rebbe Nachman goes on to say that the same applies to us; no matter how bad we feel about ourselves at any given moment, if we can find one tiny point of goodness in ourselves, we can love ourselves from that exact place.

This last teaching, I think, is a very long, mystical version of "I am strong, I am powerful." It's a message of positivity to carry us through those times when we hit the metaphorical wall, but still have a long way to go until bedtime. It's an affirmation that we may not be perfect, but we are still amazing.

I have no desire to run 26.2 miles again in this lifetime, but I'm still smack in the middle of the parenting ultramarathon. And if the mantra technique can get a middle-aged, not particularly athletic mom (that's me) through a marathon, it's definitely worth trying on a particularly crappy afternoon at home.

Say it with me:

I am strong. I am powerful.
I'm an amazing parent.

48
Good Angels and Better Devils

Yetzer hara is often translated as the "bad inclination" or "evil inclination"—but it's also the force that makes us who we are.

Sylvia had a confession to share at bedtime tonight.

"Mom? On my birthday, I was staring at my chocolate cake, and I really, really wanted to stick my finger in the frosting and lick it, but I didn't." Her birthday was six months ago.

"Great job!" I said. And I meant it.

I told her about that classic cartoon of a person walking down the street, an angel hovering above one shoulder, a devil above the other. "You listened to the angel!" I said, and she beamed.

But as I kissed her goodnight and half closed her door the way she likes it, I also felt a twinge of uncertainty about the story I'd just told her. Did I really want to teach my daughter that human impulses were divided into binaries of "good" and "bad"? Did I even believe that myself?

After all, I rarely tell my kids their behavior is "bad" (unless they've truly crossed the line and I need to make a point). The word *bad* feels too harsh and binary for most situations; instead I tend to say, "Please stop that" or "That's not okay."

Another way parents often talk about behavior is through the language of choices. A kid grabs the plastic shovel from her friend; the parent corrects them and then says, "Let's work on making better choices." This phrasing emphasizes that kids can learn to control their impulses.

Impulses: which to follow and which to resist. That's what Sylvia was talking about with her cake story; that's what the angel and devil on our shoulders represent. And Jewish tradition has also long recognized these opposing forces at work within us. The Hebrew names for these "angel" and "devil" forces are *yetzer hatov* and *yetzer hara*.

Yetzer hatov translates literally as "the good inclination": it leads us toward doing the right thing. And *yetzer hara*, literally "the bad inclination," seems on the surface to represent the exact opposite.

But while Jewish tradition recognizes these two opposing forces, it also adds a twist. Yes, the yetzer hara makes us do things we shouldn't, but according to the Talmud, it also plays an important role in human society. "Without the yetzer hara," the rabbis of the Talmud say, "no one would build a house or have children."

In other words, although yetzer hara is often translated as the "evil inclination," that's not all it is. It's also the force that makes us who we are. It makes us fully human. It's lust for power, ambition, and competitiveness; it's also the dream that things could be better than they are, the drive to reach higher. According to the rabbis, it's also the force that plants sexual desire inside us, which is sometimes—though certainly not always—a central part of baby making.

And arguably, the longing to be parents, too, is a form of desire—which often brings us our children, however they may arrive.

In other words: we wouldn't be here without the yetzer hara.

It's pretty radical to imply that we should be grateful for the devil on our shoulder. And the rabbis go even farther.

In the Torah, God begins Creation on a Sunday. At the end of most days, God pronounces the day's work *tov*, which means "good" (as in yetzer hatov). But on the sixth day, Friday, there's a change: God pronounces that day *very* good.

What's so great about Friday, the rabbis ask? And they propose this answer: that's the day the yetzer hara was created.

In other words, they're telling us that the angel on our shoulder may be good, but the devil on the other shoulder is *very* good. Or, as Mae West put it, "When I'm good, I'm very good, but when I'm bad, I'm better."

Like it or not, the yetzer hara is with us throughout our lives, and it will be with our children throughout theirs. It's an integral part of who we are as humans. Escaping it is not an option; instead, our challenge is to evolve our relationship with the yetzer hara, to harness it, to establish a healthy relationship with desire.

This isn't a skill we can ever fully perfect; it's an ongoing practice, a dance, a creative relationship. We have to teach our kids to be good, yes; but we also have to teach them to work with their yetzer hara. It's not a matter of teaching our kids to banish the devil over their shoulders, but instead, helping them to live with it.

Sylvia's working on keeping her fingers out of chocolate frosting; I'm trying to stop scrolling numbly through Twitter when I should be going to bed. I'm grateful to the ancient rabbis for reminding me that we're all on this path together—every single human on earth, no matter how young or how old.

Surrounded by good angels and better devils, learning as we go.

49
The Sweetness of Beginnings

Like Torah study, parenting is sacred work; you start
where you are, and there's no end to it.

On Friday nights, I light the Shabbat candles, cover my
eyes, and whisper the blessing. Sometimes it's a beautiful
scene, my little family standing together at the kitchen counter
as the candlelight glows. Often it's less picturesque, with one
kid whining "I'm hungry!" and the other tearing around the
kitchen at top speed. Still, this is one of my favorite moments of
the week.

Growing up, my family had candlesticks and a special
Kiddush cup, but we rarely used them. We weren't observant,
and I didn't know anyone who was. It wasn't until college that
I met an Orthodox Jewish person for the first time. We became
friends, and I pestered her with so many questions about the
traditions that she finally offered to take me home to her family
for the High Holidays. I was twenty, and it was my first time in
an Orthodox space.

When we arrived at synagogue, my friend guided me
down to the basement, where a sign read "Learner's Service."
"It'll be boring for you upstairs," she told me gently. "It's all in
Hebrew." In the learner's service, a kind man led us through
the key prayers. He sang the ancient melodies; in between,
he explained the significance of each one. He told us that the
tradition compares God to a shepherd, bringing in his flock,
counting each animal as a way of welcoming it back home. We

were that flock, he said, returning to our spiritual home on the New Year.

After services, my friend picked me up from the basement. We walked back to her house and ate the holiday lunch together at her family's beautiful, wide dining room table, with its white tablecloth and china plates.

The whole time, I was terrified I'd accidentally break a rule.

After the blessings over the bread and the wine, and after everybody had dug into her mom's matzah ball soup and brisket, to my surprise, all eyes turned to me. "How was the learner's service?" everyone wanted to know. "What did they say? Did you like it?"

I'd expected to remain silent at the meal, not to be the center of conversation! What spiritual insight could I possibly offer this family, whose members had lived such full and observant Jewish lives from birth, and who had never had a bite of bacon in their lives? I couldn't understand why they'd be curious about my experience.

Now, after studying for years myself, I realize that perhaps they saw in me what Buddhists call "beginner's mind." The sweetness and possibility of the beginning of a journey, the pure encounter of a human being with the Divine.

Becoming interested in Judaism as a young adult felt, to me, like a flame igniting inside my heart. The pilot light had been burning there for years, but as the prophet Elijah says, I was just learning to hear its "still, small voice." Now the fire was lit, and my heart glowed with love and curiosity. I had the sense of being tugged toward something—and along with tugging came a destabilization, a calling into question of much about my life.

I followed that tug to Jerusalem, then to graduate school. I learned biblical Hebrew and Talmudic Aramaic, and my beginner status faded into the past. Jewish texts and traditions became an integral part of my life, and I began to teach them.

I hadn't thought about that Rosh Hashanah dinner in years. But then Sylvia was born. As a new mom, once again a beginner in a world where everyone else seemed to be fluent, I found myself thinking back to that humbling, thrilling Rosh Hashanah experience.

I remembered that feeling of ineptness, like traveling in a foreign country where I didn't speak the language. At home, I was a functioning adult; here, I barely knew the alphabet. Though my hosts were utterly welcoming, I felt weirdly infantile.

Face-to-face with a tiny, newly arrived human being, I was similarly disoriented. I'd gone from a capable professional to an utter newbie. There were so many practical skills to learn: diapering, shushing, nursing, swaddling, how to knot the mysterious baby carrier that was just a giant piece of material. And then there were the deeper skills: calm, patience, self-confidence, being okay with mystery, and knowing what kind of crying warrants a call to the pediatrician.

Now, a few years down the road, I wish I could go back and tell myself that it's okay to be a beginner. Like Torah study, parenting is sacred work; you start where you are, and there's no end to it. Like Torah study, parenting is a beautiful expression of love, connecting us to past generations and building a bridge to the future.

If I could go back, I'd tell myself not to worry about that dizzying, disoriented state—the sweetness and possibility of the beginning of the journey. That destabilization itself can be holy, opening our hearts to what comes next.

And I'd tell myself to nurture my pilot light. To tend to that still, small voice; that glow in my heart, the same light that glows each Friday when we light the candles. We are here, together. The rest is commentary.

50

My New Mom Friend, Eve

To assume responsibility for another human being's life is an impossible task. We are responsible for our children, but we are also, ultimately, helpless.

While pregnant with Sylvia, I was in the middle of creating a musical midrash project, interpreting the stories of biblical women through indie rock songs. I'd begun this project in graduate school, and then it took on a life of its own; years later, I was still researching female biblical characters and writing songs in their voices. Sometimes it felt as if the women were speaking through me.

But I had a hard time connecting with Eve.

I loved so many other women from the Hebrew Bible: Sarah and Rachel and Esther and Vashti and Ruth . . . the list goes on. These characters dealt with family and politics and the question of how honest to be with each other and themselves. They laughed, flirted, fibbed, messed up, triumphed, and took giant risks to stand up for what they believed in. They seemed like people I might hang out with in real life.

Next to them, Eve, the first woman, had always seemed a little vague—too mythic, too abstract, too archetypal.

But as my due date approached, I began to feel a connection to Eve. After all, she'd been pregnant too. It was like when I passed another pregnant lady on the street; I spotted Eve's belly, and nodded to her with a slight smile of recognition.

In my mind, like all first-time moms, Eve and I were bonded by our shared terror and joy. Was I projecting? Absolutely. But with biblical characters, that's allowed.

In fact, projecting ourselves into the text is an important part of creating midrash.

Now that we were getting to be friends, I felt it was time to write a song about Eve. So I began to spend hours digging into her story, imagining her excitement, confusion, and fears.

I also realized something poignant about Eve's story. As the first mother, she was really, truly, on her own.

I may have felt overwhelmed sometimes, but the truth was, I was surrounded by expertise and support, both scientific and empirical. I had my mother and my midwife, along with friends who'd already had kids. I had ultrasounds and the beautiful chirp of my baby's heartbeat on the Doppler. And thanks to the internet, I had endless (sometimes overwhelming) access to advice, studies, recommendations . . . the list goes on.

Eve had none of this.

No books, no internet, no videos, no midwife, no mother.

No one had ever been pregnant before; no one had ever given birth.

I thought a lot about the loneliness of Eve's pregnancy.

After Sylvia was born, I moved on to wondering how early motherhood would have gone for Eve and her babies. I imagined her heart-shattering love for baby Cain—the first baby *ever*! I imagined her delight as Abel arrived and then as the two boys played together.

Then I thought about that moment years later, when Cain kills Abel in the field. My heart broke. And I sat down with my guitar to write a song for Eve.

As I wrote, I thought about how Eve's story connects to our own. Though her story is intensely dramatic, like most Torah stories, and written on a mythic scale, it reflects a truth that echoes through every parent's experience. To assume responsibility for another human being's life is an impossible task. We are responsible for our children, but we are, ultimately, also helpless.

It's a terrible conundrum. We parents have both too much power and too little; we are charged with keeping our children safe, yet we are powerless to do so. We are responsible for our children, yet we don't control them. How can we bear it?

One answer from Jewish tradition is that we are not alone: we are partners with God in the creation and caretaking of our children.

Whether we relate to the concept of God as a divine force, or simply a wild-card metaphor for everything we cannot control about life, this tradition feels precisely right to me. We're a big part of the picture, but there's a bigger picture beyond us, too. All we can do is accept responsibility for our part of parenting and let go of the rest.

As our kids will figure out sooner or later—ultimately, we're not in control.

I'm grateful to Judaism for this reminder that, in the end, none of us can be wholly responsible for our children. We can only do our best. And I'm grateful to Eve for helping me appreciate another, more tangible source of support: other mothers, both past and present.

Unlike the First Mother, we are lucky to be surrounded by other women who can hold us and walk beside us when it gets rough. The midwives and nurses and doctors who work to keep us safe. The moms at our same stage in the parenting journey, who know what we're dealing with. The mothers who are a few steps ahead of us and help light the way. And the long line of ancestral mothers who came before us—all the way back to Eve.

51

We Are Separate; We Are One

Recently, I've been realizing that a huge part of helping Sylvia grow up is simply taking a step back and letting her be her own person.

looked forward to Sylvia's first piano lesson for years. I was so excited to give her what my mother had given me: the gift of music.

When I was three, my mother had brought me down to the local music school for lessons. I know, that sounds high-pressure, but it really wasn't. It was fun, and mellow, and it led to a lifetime of playing music that has brought me around the world and created many of my closest friendships. It also (indirectly) led me to Aaron, who's not only my husband, but also my favorite bass player.

In short, music is one of the great loves of my life. So I was practically glowing on the day when Sylvia and I walked through the doors of the local community music school for the first time.

Unfortunately, as it turned out, Sylvia absolutely hated piano lessons. The practicing, the sticker charts, the stuffy room—all of it. For six months, she complained and cried, while I secretly dreamed of a future when she would thank me for making her stick with it.

Then, one day, I had a realization: At her age, I'd *enjoyed* violin lessons. I'd never begged to quit. And if I had? Well, my mom would have let me.

My daughter, at five, was not a mini-me reenacting my childhood. Instead, she was already a different person from me—and this person hated music lessons. Maybe they'd work for her one day, but not right now.

We quit, and everybody was immediately much happier.

Recently, I've been realizing that a huge part of helping Sylvia grow up is simply taking a step back and letting her be her own person.

When she was an infant, her physical survival depended on our near-constant attention. We fed her to keep her alive; we changed her diapers to keep her clean and healthy; we cooed and sang to her, providing stimulation for her growing brain.

Over the years, she's slowly pulled away from that extreme dependency. We're still deeply intertwined, but now she's her own person—with her own friends, her own toothpaste preferences, and her own feelings about everything from strawberries to piano lessons.

Of course, Sylvia still needs us (and we need her!). We're deeply connected, and also increasingly separate. The process of raising kids is about living in the paradox, and moving back and forth between these states.

One of the central prayers of the Jewish tradition, the Shema, also centers on these ideas of union and separation. Traditionally, this prayer bookends our days. We recite it when we wake up in the morning and when we go to bed at night.

It begins with six simple words:

Shema Yisrael, Adonai Eloheinu, Adonai echad.

Listen, people of Israel: Adonai is our God, Adonai is One.

God is One. On the surface this expresses the basic tenet of monotheism, as opposed to the polytheism out of which ancient Israelite culture grew. Read mystically, it also expresses a profound oneness or connection that underlies the separateness we all experience as we move through life. Traditionally, we chant the Shema twice a day, reminding ourselves morning and night that we are part of this great oneness.

And yet all around us, we see disconnection and separation. And in fact, the Shema prayer itself doesn't stop with oneness.

The full version continues with a list of commandments: about loving God, and marking our doorposts, and obeying the Torah's rules so that rain will come in its proper season.

In other words, immediately after its beautiful proclamation of oneness, the Shema prayer itself acknowledges that we live in a world of differentiation and separateness. In this world, we have to work to love the Divine. We can celebrate our differences as well as our commonalities, and all our choices have consequences.

Oneness and separateness, differences and commonalities, choice and consequence. These philosophical categories might sound too abstract for the nitty-gritty of parenting. But in fact, they're all intimately related to our day-to-day work as parents.

Letting Sylvia quit piano didn't mean I was failing or giving in. Instead, it meant I was recognizing her preferences (and by extension, her self) as separate from mine. Yes, there are certain things she has to do: eat her vegetables, go to school, be kind to her brother. However, music lessons are not in that category—at least, not now.

This ongoing tension between oneness and separateness reminds me of a self-help book called *Passionate Marriage* (which, incidentally, I read long before I met my husband). In it, author David Schnarch, a psychologist, portrays the back-and-forth between unity and separation as a fundamental part of healthy romantic relationships.

To back up his point, Schnarch describes an infant behavior experiment. Scientists told moms to interact naturally with their newborns; at first, mother and baby gazed into each other's eyes in peaceful unity. Then, without fail, something changed: the baby looked away, initiating a moment of separation. Only then, after reconnecting with its own self, would the baby look into its mother's eyes again.

His point, I think, was that this back-and-forth is baked into our human psychology. As he writes, "Differentiation allows each person to function independently and interdependently."

A healthy relationship involves merging and oneness—but also difference and separation. Even for infants.

We are separate; we are one. It's true with moms and babies. It's true between lovers. And the way I read the Shema prayer, it seems true between us and the Divine too.

As for Sylvia's piano lessons: we quit, waited a couple of years, then decided to give it another shot. It's going okay so far. But if she really, truly wants to stop—not just because she's hitting a roadblock, not because she doesn't want a challenge—well, I've learned my lesson. I'll give her a kiss and let her quit.

Because that's how I want to love her. Not as some projection of myself, but as her own person. Gloriously separate, even though she's mine and I am hers.

52

God, the Imperfect Parent

I find it comforting to remember that God—as described in the Torah—is impatient, imperfect, and sometimes downright pissy when faced with feisty humans.

Each year in the fall, we gather for the two holiest days of the Jewish year—Rosh Hashanah and Yom Kippur—and sing one of the most moving, compassionate prayers in the Jewish liturgy: Avinu Malkeinu.

Literally, the name means "Our Father, Our King." But I prefer to translate it more inclusively:

Our parent, our protector, have mercy on us!

Be gentle and gracious with us, even if we don't deserve it!

Ever since I was a child, I've loved this song in which we sing directly to God, acknowledging our imperfection and vulnerability, and praying for a new year of blessings rather than difficulties.

The melody I grew up with is haunting and plaintive. It's sung in a traditional scale called Freygish in klezmer music (similar to Phrygian mode, for the music-theory geeks among us).

Now that we're parents, we spend those holiday mornings in the children's service. It's generally more lighthearted and chaotic than the adult one, but still, a hush falls over the room when the leader begins Avinu Malkeinu. Each fall, our kids are bigger; each fall, Aaron and I hold them close and sing, wrapping them in our prayer shawls and swaying as we pray for life to be gentle with those we love.

When we sing to God as a metaphorical parent, we're thinking of ourselves as the children. In this context, we're appealing to an infinitely compassionate parent-version of God, who has the capacity to be kind and gracious no matter how badly we mess up. And as a helpless human, I, too, hope that the universe will be kind and compassionate to me, even speaking metaphorically.

But as a parent, I confess that this idea of acting with infinite compassion feels firmly beyond my reach. And that's why, from a parent's perspective, I actually find it comforting to remember that God—as described in the Torah—is impatient, imperfect, and sometimes downright pissy when faced with feisty humans.

Like when Korah, from the family of Levi, questions the strict leadership structure that puts his first cousins Moses and Aaron in charge of the entire Israelite nation. Does God calmly say, "Tell me more about what you're feeling"? No, God does not. Instead, God opens a giant hole in the ground and makes Korah and his entire crew fall into it.

Or take another episode, when Miriam approaches God with a similar challenge to Moses's leadership. Does God consider whether she might, in fact, have a point; that maybe Moses does have too much power? No, God does not. Instead, God strikes Miriam with leprosy and exiles her into the desert for a week. (Frustratingly, their brother Aaron, who was by Miriam's side, asking right along with her, seems to get off without punishment.)

And in the story of Noah, God destroys an entire human civilization after they behave badly. Bam: a flood covers the earth, and everyone except Noah and his family drown. A little later, God seems to regret this drastic decision, like a parent who's come down too hard on their kid. God promises not to destroy the world again and hangs a rainbow in the sky, a reminder of God's vow to do better next time.

In other words, when confronted with bad behavior, relentless questions, and even well-meaning challenges to power, sometimes God—like any parent—freaks out a little bit.

What a strange balance it is, being a parent. We are godlike in our responsibility to provide all that our children need, yet childlike when we face the power of the universe.

At once so powerful and so helpless.

The best we can do, I think, is to be gentle with ourselves. To remember that perfection is not possible, even for God.

When we mess up, as we inevitably will, we can hug our kids and apologize. Like God after the Flood, we can paint a rainbow, hang it up, and promise to try to do better.

And we can teach our kids to do the same thing. Because parents aren't the only humans who are like God. According to the Torah's creation story in Genesis, we are all created in God's image. All humans, from babies through great-grandmas.

And so we stand before each other in our power and our powerlessness—on the holiest days of the year and also on every other day. All of us made in the image of God: complicated, and huge, and beautiful, and messy, and rooted in love.

53
A Good Mom Friend Is Hard to Find

I went to meetup after meetup, but I wasn't finding mom friends; I was just making myself miserable.

Through my long and sordid quest for mom friends, I've realized something a little embarrassing: I definitely have a type.

I like the no-bullshit moms who say the things you're not supposed to say. I like the ones with messed-up hair and hand-me-down strollers and one weirdly, outlandishly fashionable element—glasses or hair or tattoos or designer sneakers.

I like the ones who knit in the summer, who laugh so loud everyone turns around to look. The ones who tell me all about their sex life, postpartum body issues, or fantasies of running off with the circus before I've even gotten their first name.

This is hard-won information; it took years of painful trial and error for me to figure out my type.

The problem was that by the time I became a mom, I had completely forgotten how to make friends the way I had in high school—simply because they happened to be in my classes. As an adult, I usually met new friends by bonding with them over a mutual obsession. At writing conferences, I met people who shared my dedication to poetry. At jam sessions, I sawed away on traditional fiddle tunes with fellow musicians, sipping Guinness and making music until the wee hours. And at the synagogue where I taught Hebrew school, I met people who shared my passion for Jewish traditions and social justice.

So when I moved across the country to Oregon, three thousand miles away from the relationships I'd built over the past decades,

I signed up for the "New-to-Town Moms" group. I had hoped that simply being moms who were new to town would magically generate its own friendships. Every couple of weeks we'd meet somewhere else: the gourmet hot cocoa store downtown, Ben & Jerry's in the suburbs, the zoo.

Together we made a stroller gaggle, a maze of wheeled buggies that blocked other customers from getting to the cashier. "Sorry!" we'd say, shaking our heads when our toddlers grabbed strangers' legs with their sticky hands. "Thanks!" we'd say apologetically when someone returned a rattle one of our babies had flung across the room.

We probably looked like a sweet little community. We sipped our hot cocoa, ate our ice cream with spoons so it wouldn't drop on our babies' heads, all the while pulling wipes and loveys and small plastic containers of pretzels out of our bags, like magicians practicing on a lunch break.

From the outside, I thought, we must have seemed like those moms who'd been together since birth class, now raising our little ones as a community—not cousins, but *practically* cousins. But that wasn't how I experienced it. To me, it felt like hanging out with a group of strangers.

Let me be clear: there was absolutely nothing wrong with any of these moms. In fact, they were great: friendly, interesting, kind, and welcoming. If we'd worked side by side, or been roommates, or been able to talk uninterrupted for more than three minutes, I bet we'd have become friends for real.

But as I struggled to make friends in this context, I began to realize that drinking hot cocoa with a group of near strangers during the forty-five-minute window between naptime and the next diaper change . . . wasn't working for me.

In the end, I had to admit to myself that going to the meetup was making me more lonely than staying at home. I wasn't finding mom friends; I was just making myself miserable. I quit going and reconciled myself to being pretty much alone—besides Aaron and our baby—for quite a while.

That was a difficult time. Looking back, I don't know where postpartum despair ended and my general feeling of distance, alienation, and aloneness began. I'd never realized how much I relied on my friends and family to reflect me back to myself. Now, across the country, I sometimes felt I was slipping away like a balloon.

As hard as it was, I'm grateful for the lessons of that time. In that dark place, I learned to love myself in a way I had never needed to before—not depending on anyone outside myself for validation but finding that basic acceptance within myself.

And I am grateful to report that my quest for mom friends eventually bore fruit. Much like dating, I had to give up on finding "the one(s)" before I actually found them. I'd resigned myself to a monastically lonely Portland existence, but over time, I slowly began to collect true friends.

Some of them aren't moms at all. As my kids get a little older, and I'm able to leave the house more, my life begins to revert to the way it was before—when friendship was not about lining up with a specific peer group at a specific stage of life, but about who you resonate with, who makes you laugh.

But some of them are, in fact, mom friends, right here where I live. Classic, tell-it-like-it-is, poop-and-all mom friends. I met them one by one, over the years, not in scheduled meetups, but over the course of living my daily life. One at a potluck brunch for a babysitting co-op that neither of us ended up joining. One on a film set. A few at our kids' Hebrew school—a special treat, because we can have Passover and Shabbat together. One in my own backyard, while she was visiting our next-door neighbor. And more too—beautiful, wonderful, weird, quirky moms, just the way I like them.

You know who you are. I love you. You were worth the wait.

54
Back and Forth: On Angels and Ambivalence

Like angels, we are in constant motion. We bridge impossible contradictions. We hold the world together.

Before I became a mom, I could *sort of* imagine the earth-shattering love I'd one day have for my kids. I couldn't quite predict how it would inflate my heart to encompass the entire planet. And I didn't expect to find myself looking at our baby, insisting urgently to Aaron, "No, you don't understand, I mean she *literally* looks like an angel!" But I did expect to desperately love my baby.

What I could not have imagined were the other, less socially acceptable feelings that sometimes accompanied this earth-shattering love. Complex feelings of frustration, loss, and loneliness associated with motherhood, which psychologists call "maternal ambivalence" (or more inclusively, "parental ambivalence").

Maternal ambivalence? Pre-baby, I'd have felt pretty certain that would not describe me. Maybe *other* people would experience ambivalence toward their own kids—but not me. After all, wouldn't that make me . . . a bad mom?

Luckily, psychology says no. According to experts, maternal ambivalence is a natural part of parenting, and we all experience it to one degree or another. So why are the difficult parts of parenting (not the poop and the sleep deprivation, but the deep emotional struggles) still surrounded by an aura of shame?

Psychiatrist Barbara Almond, whose research helped bring mixed feelings about motherhood into the light, compared this shame to Oscar Wilde's description of his queerness as "the love that dare not speak its name." (Wilde was, in fact, quoting a poem by his lover, Lord Alfred Douglas.)

Almond argued that society's repression of maternal ambivalence in our time is comparable to the repression of queer love in Douglas and Wilde's: "Everyone feels it, but has trouble talking about it, and those who do speak up raise feelings of alarm in those who are pushing these feelings out of consciousness."

What, exactly, is ambivalence? The *Oxford English Dictionary* calls it the "coexistence in one person of contradictory emotions or attitudes (as love and hatred) towards a person or thing." The same dictionary also offers a "literary" definition, which is more fluid and less binary, defining ambivalence as "oscillation, fluctuation, and variability."

I'm intrigued by this variable understanding of ambivalence, and how this image of fluidity resonates with the prophet Ezekiel's vision of God. In his mystical testimony, Ezekiel describes angels with four faces flying to and fro, from one side to another, "speeding back and forth like flashes of lightning."

Oscillation, fluctuation, variability.

Jewish mystics see this back-and-forth movement as central to the nature of existence. Back and forth, in Ezekiel's Hebrew, is *ratzo v'shov*, often translated as "run and return."

This is a vision of existence as a woven fabric; just as a loom has warp and weft, x-axis and y-axis, existence itself is pulled tightly in two directions.

Me and you, death and life, positive and negative, child and parent. You can't have one without the other.

This vision of a world in which everything is intrinsically linked to its opposite can help us hold a more expansive vision of parenthood. One that can, by its very nature, contain opposites, ambiguities, and ambivalence.

A vision in which we can be both overwhelmed with love and strung out with exhaustion. A parenting practice where we can honor our dedication to our kids by taking time away from them when needed, so that we can return as better parents. A conception of parenthood that accepts, rather than denies, the complicated emotions that accompany this profound experience.

We run toward our children, and we also need to return to ourselves. We are one, and we also are separate.

Ezekiel's angels are not the cherubs of Renaissance paintings, chubby and ruddy, static in their radiance. They are something else entirely: paradoxical, complex, hard-working. Going back and forth and back and forth, keeping the fabric of existence taut.

They are, in short, like mothers.

And maybe we are like angels. We are in constant motion. We bridge impossible contradictions. We hold the world together.

55
Debate for the Sake of Heaven

Differing opinions don't have to reflect antagonism; instead, they can be a sign of partnership and respect.

I never expected parenting skills to be a Hunger Games–style arena for debate. Even the experts don't agree on the basics. Sleep training, sugar, screen time, discipline: it's easy to find doctors (and parents) who argue one approach with the utmost conviction, and just as many who will take up arms for the exact opposite.

Having spent a fair amount of time studying Torah, this feels familiar to me, because disagreements are an honored part of Jewish tradition. These disagreements, often centered around how to interpret ancient texts, are philosophical on the one hand, but also have practical ramifications—much like the question of whether to co-sleep, or breast milk versus formula.

There's even a special name for this kind of sacred debate: *machloket.*

I was in my last year of college when I first heard that word. I'd been feeling some curiosity about my Jewish heritage, and a friend suggested I check out an open study session that took place on Wednesday nights in the philosophy building. I worked up my courage, headed across campus on a chilly fall night, and climbed the marble stairs, my footsteps echoing.

I was a few minutes late, and the heavy wooden doors were closed when I arrived. When I opened them, I was expecting to encounter the monastic quiet of our university library. Instead, a wild hubbub of voices and movement greeted me.

I crept into the room and saw five long tables filled with students sitting across from each other in pairs. I watched as they spoke excitedly across the tables at each other, gesturing and exclaiming over the large books that lay open between them.

I must have looked lost, because a skinny guy in a yarmulke walked up to me and said, kindly, "First time?"

When I nodded, he introduced himself as a student organizer and explained the basics to me. This partner-style study was called *chavruta* learning, from the word *friend* in Hebrew, and this was the traditional way of learning Jewish texts.

A chavruta, he told me, is a pair of partners who work together to unravel the text—to translate it, to unpack it, and to push each other to understand it more deeply. Challenging your chavruta is an important part of studying together. And often, at the center of the texts we study is machloket—sacred argument.

Intense debate, in this system, is not an insult; it's a mark of respect for the subject and for your opponent.

And the good debates last forever. As the rabbis say in *Pirkei Avot* (*Ethics of the Fathers*) 5:17, "Every machloket that is for the sake of heaven is destined to endure." In other words, when it's a deep, solid, good-arguments-on-both-sides disagreement, the debate itself is worth holding onto.

Many of our traditional texts still preserve arguments between scholars who lived two thousand years ago. For example, Rabbis Hillel and Shammai. A famous pair of rabbis with diametrically opposed worldviews, they spent their lives debating their antithetical interpretations of Jewish ethics and law. Though Hillel almost always "wins," in that his opinion becomes law, the text carefully preserves Shammai's opinion, too, out of respect. And to this day, we study Shammai's views right alongside Hillel's, as if to say: even if one person is right, you can't really know the truth without hearing both sides.

When I was pregnant with Sylvia, I started to read books about birth and infant care. I quickly found myself overwhelmed with a flood of contrary opinions. Which was safer, home birth or hospital birth? What was better for the baby, co-sleeping or a crib? And was sleep training a great idea or a traumatizing mistake?

Standing in the parenting section of the bookstore, I thought back to the wild hubbub of that boisterous Jewish learning session. I had to smile, imagining a bunch of child-rearing experts gesturing at each other, pointing to their proof texts from Dr. Sears and Wendy Mogel, raising their voices in rabbinic-style machloket.

In Jewish tradition, these opposing arguments are preserved together in the same text. In the bookstore or online, though, each expert sticks to their own website, book, article, or video. Rarely do they engage in what our tradition calls "machloket for the sake of heaven"—the back-and-forth, push-and-pull conversation, where each side acknowledges that the other has a point and that the truth probably lies somewhere in between.

I think the parenting debates could learn a thing or two from these ancient Jewish scholarly traditions. Differing opinions don't have to reflect antagonism; instead, they can be a sign of partnership and respect. Multiple voices and opinions can coexist in a single room and on a single page. That way, we could consider all the sides of an argument before taking that final step, which ultimately we have to do on our own: consider what the experts on both sides have to say, and then find the parenting path that works for us.

56

Please Don't Yell at Us, God!

It's the prayer of a kid who just got busted sneaking Halloween candy into their room—or an adult who knows that we are all deeply flawed.

One morning I went into Sylvia's bedroom and noticed a new piece of "art" on the wall: a self-portrait just above her pillow, painstakingly drawn onto the pale-yellow wall in black permanent marker.

Sylvia was eating breakfast at the kitchen table, and from where I stood in her bedroom, I could hear her humming happily to herself.

I stood there, frozen in place by simultaneous and contradictory impulses. Part of me felt absolutely certain I needed to call Sylvia in immediately and tell her that she'd really crossed the line. There was no easy fix: it was going to take two coats of primer, plus more yellow paint, whatever shade that was . . . basically, a giant pain.

The other part of me wanted to laugh out loud and hug her. In the self-portrait, she'd drawn her eyes as large as saucers; her hair sprouted out of her head in all directions; her mouth was a giant U-shaped smile, and there was a carefully drawn heart below her face, close to where her own real heart would be. In short, it was adorable.

Standing there, held precisely between the impulse to yell and the impulse to hug, I understood in a new way what the Jewish mystics mean when they say there is a cosmic balance between compassion, chesed, and judgment, gevurah, the two primary and opposing elements of divine (and human) energy. In that moment, I experienced a perfect real-world example.

The part of me that wanted to hug Sylvia for her exuberant artwork was the side of chesed—the warmth of loving-kindness, generosity, and joy. The part that wanted to give her a time-out for drawing on the wall in permanent marker was gevurah—hard, cold boundaries, consequences, and limits.

We as parents are constantly balancing chesed and gevurah in figuring out the right response toward our kids' behavior. And according to Jewish tradition, God (metaphorically understood as a parent) is carrying out the same process toward us (metaphorically understood as God's children).

This process takes center stage around Rosh Hashanah and Yom Kippur, when God determines how our coming year will unfold. During these holiest days of the Jewish year, we explicitly try to invoke God's chesed over gevurah by reciting the Thirteen Attributes of Mercy, characteristics drawn from biblical sources describing God's merciful actions in the world. Over and over, we repeat these thirteen attributes throughout the liturgy, begging God repeatedly to act with compassion, to be "slow to anger."

Which is to say, in human terms—Please don't yell at us, God! Forgive us, even if we've misbehaved terribly.

It's the prayer of a kid who just got busted sneaking Halloween candy into their room—or an adult who knows that we are all deeply flawed.

When I think back to that moment in Sylvia's room, deciding what to do next, it occurs to me: if we adults spend our holiest days praying for God to access compassion rather than anger, then we, too, should probably try to err on the side of chesed in our parenting.

Not that we shouldn't have boundaries; gevurah is important too. Still, two thousand years of wisdom is worth listening to. The rabbis urge us—as we urge God—to lean toward the right side, to err on the side of compassion over judgment.

Even in a difficult parenting moment, when everything in me wants to unloose full gevurah energy on my kid, part of my job is to remember that I have a choice. I have to balance that gevurah with chesed.

In the case of Sylvia's self-portrait, her permanent-marker-on-the-wall art was so freaking cute—those saucer-sized eyes, that adorable, spiky hair—that it was easy for me to hold on to my love for her, while also knowing there had to be some sort of consequence.

My hope is that even when it's a less cute transgression, I can still act toward my kids as we ask the Divine to act toward us on Rosh Hashanah and Yom Kippur. We, too, mess up all the time, even if we cover up the evidence better.

So here is my parenting prayer. To open my heart; to lean toward chesed; to see God's face in my children's faces and in my own. Even when that face is crudely drawn. Even when I know I'm going to have to paint over it later.

57
Keep Growing

As our kids begin to grow up, we may experience
a sense of loss for their teeny selves. But that's part of
the deal: letting go of their previous versions as they
blossom into new ones.

The older Sylvia gets, the more adamant she is that she will *never* grow up. In fact, she recently founded her own no-grownups-allowed empire, "Kidonia," with her treehouse as its capital.

But as with Neverland, no one can stay in Kidonia forever; eventually, we all grow up. And that's a good thing. As our kids begin to grow up, we may experience a sense of loss, even grief, for their teeny selves. But that's part of the deal: letting go of their previous versions as they blossom into new ones.

And that's why I always wince when I see people post pictures of their adorable kids with the hashtag #stopgrowing.

Part of it is that I secretly feel bad about wanting them to keep growing. Because yes, little squishies are adorable, but I personally experience even more joy with them as they grow older.

When Elijah, at age two, started coming into my bed every two hours all night long—at the same moment that Sylvia, age four, developed night terrors and woke up screaming during the times when Elijah was actually sleeping—did I want them to #stopgrowing? No, I did not. I desperately wanted them to #growoutofit.

I will never again take sleeping for granted, and one of the great joys of my life as my kids exit toddlerhood is being able to talk to a friend for ten minutes without worrying about where they are.

But to be perfectly honest, my real issue with #stopgrowing —and the reason it makes me so uncomfortable—is that underneath the exhaustion, part of me secretly wants them to stop growing too. Sometimes I *do* wish this moment could last forever: I live with the people I love the most, and our house is filled with whoops of delight and cute little sandals and sweetly awkward hand-drawn portraits.

But that's not how it works. Sooner or later we have to accept the fact that time changes us, as David Bowie sings so perfectly in the chorus of "Changes."

We are all students in the classroom of life—we, our elders, and our little ones, even David Bowie. We live in the medium and the matrix of time, with its strange changes, its untraceable movement.

Listen: I'm not really suggesting we boycott #stopgrowing. It isn't hurting anyone, which is more than I can say about most of the internet. I know it really just means "Look how adorable these little peanuts are! I love them so much."

Still, something in me wishes that we could instead embrace #keepgrowing.

Not just for our kids, but also for us. We, too, are told that growing older is bad, that we need to filter away the signs. Instead of accepting the passage of time, and the wisdom that often accompanies it, we're encouraged to hold on to our younger selves with a death grip.

So #keepgrowing feels like a blessing we could give to each other—and to our children.

May we keep growing into new versions of ourselves. Keep discovering new interests, new abilities, new stories, new friends.

May we keep growing our hearts toward more compassion— sometimes through moments of cuteness, sometimes through the inevitable difficulties and heartbreak.

May we keep learning more about who we are, increasing our curiosity about the world around us.

May we keep finding new ways to love each other and understand each other more deeply as we grow and change, as long as we have the privilege of being here in this house—here on this earth—together.

PART 5

Moving On

Every Ending Contains a Beginning

58

Why God Created Mothers

This capable, all-seeing, godlike mother-self doesn't just appear the instant a baby arrives. At least for me, it took a while to grow into.

I love the old Yiddish saying "God couldn't be everywhere—so God created mothers."

Okay, so there may be a bit of the overbearing-Jewish-mother stereotype in this expression (mothers are *everywhere*! they're *watching you*!). But I prefer to understand the phrase as a tribute, an acknowledgment of the ways in which we mothers are actually somewhat . . . divine.

We're human, too, of course. We need support and rest, just like anyone else. But we also are a little bit transcendent, with our magical powers of comforting and soothing, our wildly expanded hearts.

This capable, all-seeing, godlike mother-self doesn't just appear the instant a baby arrives, though. Well, maybe it does for some. But for me, it took a while to grow into.

At first, after becoming a mother, I tried desperately to hold on to the person I'd been before. But much as I tried to cling, pieces of my pre-baby self kept drifting out of reach. I watched them float away, helpless and confused, as I held my new baby with my new, postpartum body.

I didn't know then that there was actually a word, invented by anthropologist Dana Raphael in 1973, for what was happening. She called it *matrescence*: the "self-birthing" of becoming a mother.

(Sidenote: Raphael also introduced another word to the English birth lexicon: When she struggled with breastfeeding her first child and expressed the wish for more support at home so she could focus on caring for her infant, an older Greek woman told her, "We call that a *doula*." Raphael realized that we needed that word and especially that role of supporting birthing women and new mothers in our culture as well.)

The word *matrescence* intentionally carries echoes of *adolescence*, that other great developmental transition. Both involve a magnificent blossoming into a new stage but also a leaving behind of the previous one. To become mothers, we have to let go of our pre-mother selves, just as when we became young adults, we had to relinquish our child-selves forever.

This all sounds very theoretical, but, in fact, modern brain science has begun to support what Raphael and I (and so many mothers) have experienced.

Scientists have demonstrated actual physiological transformation in the brains of new moms that prime the brain for dramatic change. These changes are especially strong in the regions that allow us to perceive emotions and mental states in others.

In other words, matrescence makes us more aware of those around us, more empathetic, more tuned-in. And this applies to those who have not given birth too; many experts now understand matrescence as a developmental state that applies to everyone who becomes a parent.

Which brings me back to that Yiddish saying. "God couldn't be everywhere, so God created mothers." We are godlike in our ability to connect; we are godlike in the depth of our love as we watch over our children and the world.

No one is *born* a mother. However we arrive, becoming a mother is an act of creation—another birth. And like any birth, it's both joyful and difficult, with an undercurrent of pain running beneath the river of joy.

Maybe God, too, feels this strange mixture of loss and joy, the loneliness of responsibility, the privilege and burden of empathy. Maybe that's really why God created mothers—not because God couldn't be anywhere, but rather to have some company.

Someone who understands, as we mothers do, what it's like to hold the world together with love.

59
Finding Our Own Paths

It's sweet to think of my daily interactions with Sylvia and Elijah reverberating even into their old age, when I'm long gone from the planet. But it scares me too.

I found the power of my kids' early years both empowering and terrifying. On the one hand, I felt good when I helped them begin to build the skills that would serve them for the rest of their lives—like saying "You're okay," instead of freaking out when they took a minor spill and were clearly fine; to teach resilience. I had the wonderful sense that this tiny muscle I was helping them develop ("I fell, but I'm okay!") would serve them well in the years to come.

On the other hand, when my own bad habits were on display, I worried that I was subtly imprinting them on my kids. When they watched me standing at the kitchen counter, compulsively scrolling on my phone, I wondered: was I laying the groundwork for an unhealthy relationship with technology?

That concern wasn't *just* me being paranoid; the first few years of life are important in countless ways. A peek at Harvard's childhood development site, for example, tells me that "healthy development in the early years (particularly birth to three) provides the building blocks for educational achievement, economic productivity, responsible citizenship, lifelong health, strong communities, and successful parenting of the next generation."

Dang . . . . So if I'm reading this correctly, how I handle the first few years of my kid's life might determine their own parenting skills? I'm not only affecting whether *they* get into Harvard, but whether their *kids* do?

(Just kidding about the Harvard part—they rejected my college application, by the way—but not about the pressure of finding out that my kids' first few years could influence their own "successful parenting.")

As my kids exit early childhood, I may have less imprinting power, but I'm even more aware of the impact of my actions on them. I can see how the way Aaron and I run our household is becoming part of how they see the world. This is true both of the practices we require of them (clean your room at least once a week, move your body every day, eat reasonably healthy) and the values we teach (it's okay to love whomever you want, we don't make fun of people who are different, it's important to stand up for what's right).

The book of Proverbs, too, understands the power we have to affect our children's lives. "Train up a child in the way they should go," the proverb says, "and when they are old, they will not depart from it" (Proverbs 22:6). Our power to "train up a child" isn't limited to the first years of their lives; it continues for years. And, according to this wisdom text, our parenting will continue to affect our kids even when they are elderly.

It's sweet to think of my daily interactions with Sylvia and Elijah reverberating even into their old age, when I'm long gone from the planet. But it scares me too.

If I mess up now, will it haunt them for the rest of their lives?

To be clear, I am aware that thinking this way is extremely unhelpful. Of *course* I'm going to mess up; that's part of being a human parent, which is definitely better than, say, a robot parent.

That's why I prefer a different translation of this proverb. Another, equally valid, interpretation of the original Hebrew is much more reassuring. It states: "Educate a child in a way that respects their nature, and when they are old, they will not depart from it."

Rather than forcing our children to adapt to the world (the way they should go), this interpretation asks us, instead, to focus on respecting the child in front of us. In this framework, the most essential skill I can teach my kids is not how to "succeed" but how to know themselves. How to love themselves.

And since the best way to teach is by example, this challenges me to model self-knowledge and self-love by *parenting* in a way that respects my own nature.

Just like our kids, we are differently abled, differently gifted, differently wired. It's worth stopping once in a while to consider: How can we parent in a way that works for us? Are there things we could let go of, or adapt, in order to sweeten the experience?

One tiny example from my own life: since my own amazing mother had always been involved with our public school PTA, I'd always expected to do the same with my kids' schools. So I signed up. I went to meetings. I did . . . stuff. I sort of hated it, and definitely didn't feel like I was contributing in any significant way, but it didn't occur to me to quit.

Then a fellow mom friend casually mentioned one day that she'd never been involved in PTA. "Just not my thing," she said. Hearing her say that, I realized that it wasn't *my* thing either. Yes, I liked the idea of supporting the school, but it just wasn't working for me. I quit, and I've never regretted it, and I don't think they particularly miss me either.

Sure, a lot of parenting involves just sucking it up and doing the work. But what if we could also, when it works, adjust the job of parenting to our own nature? What better way to teach our children the value of respecting their own paths than to find a way to walk our own?

In the end, this is what I hope my kids will carry into their old age: the knowledge of who they are. The knowledge that I love them, and that I want them to love themselves too.

60

Jungle Gyms and Oxen: Where the Ancient Laws of Damages Meet the Playground

What exactly is within my control? Where's that perfect balance between caution and hypervigilance?

When my husband, Aaron, was ten, he fell off a jungle gym and broke his arm while showing off for a girl on the playground. (Typical.)

Before we had kids, this story would come up only rarely, usually because of some small household task requiring arm rotation. "Gotta do this one with my left arm," he'd say cheerfully. "Did I ever tell you the story about the time I fell off the jungle gym?" To which I'd answer, "Yes, a few times."

Now, I get to hear this story retold regularly at dinner; one of our kids requests it every couple of months. Partly because Aaron is a great storyteller; mostly because they love nothing more than hearing about their dad getting hurt while doing something stupid. Their delight is endless.

As he whips them into a frenzy with tales of his ill-advised acrobatics, I interrupt every few minutes to interject, "And *that's* why you need to be careful on the jungle gym." My kids think I'm missing the point of the story. What they don't understand is that to me, being careful *is* the point of the story.

Oh, the constant balance between trying to keep kids physically safe and letting them push the boundaries of what they can do.

The truth is that despite my admonitions, I know that taking risks is intrinsic to having a meaningful life. And no matter how careful I am to instill prudent jungle-gym behavior in my kids, injuries, too, are part of life (*pupupu*). Even if we never left the house, my kids would find a way to scale the bookshelves, slide down the banister, or jump off the bunk bed and break something. All I can do is control what I can control and let the rest be.

But what exactly is within my control? Where's that perfect balance between caution and hypervigilance?

There is an entire body of ancient Jewish law in the Talmud that relates to these questions, delving into how we should deal with damages and injuries, how to determine when people are responsible for damage, and when it's just the result of bad luck.

On the surface, many of the Talmud's examples seem to have little to do with daily life today. Oxen gore neighbors, people accidentally fall into open wells, and cows trample neighbors' vegetable fields.

But looking more deeply, this body of laws about how to stay safe—and what to do if an injury does happen—feels very relevant to me as the parent of a freewheeling kid (Elijah, age four) who doesn't quite understand that he's subject to the law of gravity.

The rabbis begin this section of the Talmud—called Nezikin, which means "damages"— by categorizing various types of damage, essentially scanning the world for sources of injury and harm. This is a familiar move to anyone who's gone out in the world with a toddler; looking for potential pitfalls is just part of the deal. Even at the neighborhood park, it's easy to identify a bunch of them: collision trajectories with swings, someone else's half-eaten sandwich on a bench, twelve-year-olds on BMX bikes careening down every available hill.

After the rabbis are done categorizing the everyday dangers of the world, they move on to a more nuanced question: which damages are predictable enough to be someone's fault, and which are more like freak accidents?

For example: If my unleashed dog runs across the street and bites you, that's on me. But if I'm flying a kite at the beach, and the wind picks it up and drops it on your fancy picnic, ruining your lemon meringue pie—not really my fault.

The practical reason behind these categories is to determine, when damage occurs, whether and how much we need to compensate each other. But there's a deeper question here, too, one that goes back to the balance between vigilance and risk: Where does our ability to control the world end? And how far does our responsibility extend to keep each other safe?

In Nezikin, the rabbis seem to say: Our job is to prevent the clear dangers we can foresee. Beyond that, there's nothing we can do.

The rabbis wrote these ideas down almost two thousand years ago, and probably passed them on orally for centuries before that. This reminds me that negotiating risk is not a modern issue. The tension between helicopter parenting and free-range parenting isn't new, not exactly. It's about mitigating risk, an essential part of being human, and we all have to deal with it in one way or another.

None of us knows what is going to happen; this is part of what it means to be alive. It can be anxiety-provoking, but it's also joyful. Because along with the possibility of damage and risk, the future also holds the delight of surprises.

Meeting a new mom friend at a park leads to an unexpected epic hang.

Strolling past a box of newborn kittens leads to an adorable new member of the household.

And there's the experience I had a couple of weeks ago, when Sylvia pulled off a sketchy jungle-gym maneuver before I could tell her it wasn't safe. "That's how your dad broke his arm," I might have said, but I'm so glad I didn't. She caught herself, grinned at me, and raised her eyebrows in astonishment at her success.

I smiled back at her. She's getting stronger before my eyes, growing up. She's starting to face the world, with all its risks and joys, on her own terms.

61
Every Family Has Its Own Torah

Our Jewish lives change over time, ebbing and flowing.
Some years, Jewish practice might feel more distant;
other years, it might take center stage.

There is no delight like the delight of my children coming home from brunch with my parents to report, gleefully, "We ate *bacon*!!!!"

Our family policy is that we don't eat pork in the house, but when the kids aren't with us—for example, out to brunch with their grandparents—they are free to make their own decisions.

Is that policy strictly kosher? Uh, no. But it works for us.

There's a wild variety of ways to live Jewishly. There are nearly infinite expressions of religious Judaism, and the same goes for cultural Judaism; combine the two, and the possibilities are endless.

This rainbow palette of Judaisms resonates, for me, with the mystical tradition that each of our souls is linked to a specific letter of the Torah scroll. Not just a letter of the alphabet, but a specific letter within a specific word that resonates with our souls and represents something fundamental about who we are.

I love how this tradition roots each of us—personally, privately—in our shared Torah, while also conveying the incredible multiplicity of our relationships to Jewish tradition. There are hundreds of thousands of ways to live Jewishly, and we each have the freedom to find the expression of Judaism that works for us.

This goes for families too: every family has its own way of expressing Jewishness. I love witnessing this in my work as a b'nei mitzvah guide for unaffiliated families. Some of the families I work with balk at any traditional religious observance but enjoy creating their own rituals around meals, vacations, and holidays. Others bake challah every Friday and play soccer every Saturday. Some keep kosher to honor their cultural heritage but are allergic to the word *God*. And still others are deeply spiritual but connect to the Divine most easily through meditation or nature.

In daily life, these families are happy with their level of Jewish practice; it works for them. But as we embark on the b'nei mitzvah process together, they often express anxiety about how to do it "right." Suddenly they worry that their family isn't "religious enough" or "educated enough," that it won't be an "official" bar/bat/b'nei mitzvah.

I get it; sacred ceremonies are a big deal, and tradition holds so much weight. And there's an understandable anxiety about throwing a big family celebration centered on religion when your family identity is nowhere near "religious" (and maybe even resolutely "not religious").

This is where I like to come back to the tradition of our own Torah letters. To me, it means that the Torah belongs to all of us equally, and is incomplete without each of us. Not some idealized extra-holy-super-Jew version of ourselves, but exactly as we are, with all our questions and struggles, our inconsistencies, our deeply held certainties.

Each of us is a single letter in the scroll, one dot in the pointillist masterpiece that is our existence as a people. And for some of these dots, bacon is just part of a delicious brunch.

In Hebrew calligraphy, the letters of Torah are sometimes described as flickering flames. If you've ever peeked inside a Torah scroll, you'll understand why; many of the letters bulge toward the top, then grow narrow, just like a candle.

Like flames, we are not static. Individuals change; families change. We grow, attenuate, blossom, fracture. We move through different stages and relationships with our heritage, our traditions, our culture, and the Divine.

Our Jewish lives, too, change over time, ebbing and flowing. Some years, Jewish practice might feel more distant; other years, it can take center stage as a crucial element of family life. And the beautiful thing is that the traditions remain there for us, whether we're accessing them at the moment or not.

As modern Jewish families, we have the incredible privilege of choosing which traditions make sense to us. Some criticize this approach as "buffet Judaism," implying that we should adapt ourselves to religious laws rather than taking what works for us.

But personally, I don't see what's wrong with a buffet. Spiritually speaking, there's room at the table for vegans and meat lovers, mystics and behaviorists, passionate devotees of the Divine and hardcore atheists.

Like all the best buffets, this can be a smorgasbord of foodways. There are flavors for all seasons, dishes remembered from childhood or discovered as adults. It's a plentiful feast that is always there for us when we're hungry for it, even if we've been away for a long time.

Just as there is no ideal version of a family, there is there is no ideal version of a family's relationship with Judaism. The important thing is to show up, with love, in a way that makes sense to us. To be generous, honest, and patient with each other and ourselves. To hold on to what we need at the moment, and let the rest go gracefully, knowing we will find it when it's time, if that's our path.

The Torah's letters flicker; they dance; our interpretation of them changes. Here we are—each person, each family, each in our own unique way—and here they are, after three thousand years, still holding us in their light.

62
Parenting Rituals, Old and New

One ritual at a time, these milestones mark the weeks, months, and years connecting us to the past as we hurtle toward the future.

The samovar my husband's great-grandmother carried across Russia sits on top of our bookshelf. Its squat, sturdy shape is strangely reminiscent of the sepia photos of my own squat, sturdy Russian great-grandmother. Every time I look at it, I feel a warm, dizzying sense of connection across time and space to these two women I've never met—my own great-grandmother and Aaron's.

On Friday nights, when I light Shabbat candles on our kitchen counter and see their glow reflected in my children's eyes, I feel a similarly profound power, knowing that mothers have been seeing their babies' faces lit up by this warmth for over two thousand years.

This is the magic of rituals and traditions—whether cultural, religious, or some combination of the two.

Ritual connects us to our ancestors, but it's not static; culture changes and traditions adapt. (Case in point: we don't use the samovar to make tea.) Sometimes we innovate on ancient rituals; other times, we simply make up new ones to meet the needs of our moment.

As a child, growing up, I loved to make herbal potions in our backyard, mixing water, red clover, black walnuts, ivy leaves, and a shake of baby powder in a Dixie cup. (No, I didn't drink it.) Only later, as I began to learn about plant medicine, did I realize that without knowing it, I was instinctively taking part in a traditional ritual of connection with the natural world.

Later, in college, I became increasingly interested in my Jewish heritage. Attending student Shabbat services didn't really work for me. So I decided to do what I could in my dorm room. I lit tea lights and recited the blessing over the candles; I recited the Hamotzi prayer over potato chips and the wine blessing over apple juice. Was this the official, kosher version of the ritual? No. But it worked; I was marking Friday nights as a sacred time.

As the years went on, I studied Jewish texts and traditions until I was able to step fully into the prayers and rituals. For a long time, this worked perfectly. But as I began to teach and later officiate, I found that sometimes the traditional rituals were not enough.

When families started asking me to officiate at b'nei mitzvah, Jewish tradition offered plenty of guidance. But when people came to me for ritual support after a breakup, or at the beginning of a new job, or while struggling with a major life decision, I needed to innovate.

In these moments, I found that my childhood potion making served as good training for the adult practice of creating my own rituals, using fire, water, plants, and words.

These are powerful ceremonial tools, which work whether rituals are ancient or new, communal or personal. In the traditional *havdalah* ceremony, we sip wine, smell sweet spices, light a candle with multiple wicks, and observe the reflection of flames on our fingertips as we mark the end of the Sabbath. When a bat mitzvah student got her period for the first time and wanted to honor the occasion, I used flower petals, red candies, raspberry leaves, and a pitcher of water poured over her feet to help her celebrate this new stage in her life.

Making up rituals may sound distant from normative Jewish tradition, but in fact the practice is nothing new or unique. Around the globe and across millennia, Jews (and in particular, Jewish women) have created ceremonial rituals to mark time and ease transitions. Most don't appear in prayer books or other sacred texts, which were written and compiled by men; yet they have played an important part in women's daily lives.

For example, in western European Ashkenazi communities, the lemony *etrog* fruit, part of the Sukkot harvest festival, was also used as an aid in fertility and childbearing. In some North African communities, women and girls marked the seventh night of Hanukkah with special gatherings at which they'd eat cakes, celebrate the New Moon, and tell the tale of Judith, an ancient heroine whose story is connected to Hanukkah. And in eastern Europe, when a woman's labor began, all the other women in the house would take their hair down and untie any knots in the house to help the birth go smoothly. (I wish I'd known about that; maybe it would have helped with my own births.)

Since I became a parent, ritual has been a consistent source of support. To welcome Sylvia, we had a *brit habat*, literally, a "daughter's covenant." A beloved rabbi came to our Brooklyn apartment to dab olive oil on Sylvia's forehead, drip water on her teeny toes, read prayers, and offer her wise, queer, feminist blessing.

Two years later, when Elijah was born on the other side of the country, we went with a traditional circumcision ceremony. A mohel with a long beard did his thing, our local Reconstructionist rabbi offered a blessing, and a number of our closest family and (mostly non-Jewish) friends gathered around, looking extremely nervous, but loving and supporting us as a family.

Both of these rituals surrounded us with community at a moment when we were in transition. And ritual continues to support us, carrying us forward as our kids grow older.

On Friday evenings, just after lighting the candles, I say the traditional parent's blessing for Sylvia and Elijah. They squirm and protest as I whisper and kiss their foreheads, but I love this sweet moment in the week. And they've added their own ritual, whispering into my ear afterward—sometimes gibberish, sometimes "I love you so much, Mom."

One day not so far in the future, they'll each begin preparing for their b'nei mitzvah, to mark their transition out of childhood (insert crying emoji). One ritual at a time, these milestones mark the weeks, months, and years connecting us to the past as we hurtle toward the future.

For now, though, my children are still firmly in childhood. I still get to tuck them in at bedtime. We each name one thing we're grateful for, and then I sing them the Shema prayer, as so many parents have over the centuries. I give them each a kiss and turn out the light. I go downstairs, where the samovar still sits on the bookshelf, as if nothing at all has changed.

63

The Infinite, Mystical Power of *Teshuvah* as a Parent

The world is constantly being created, and so is teshuvah. Always available, always ready.

P arenting has a way of magically revealing to us the places where we're . . . less than perfect. In the harsh light of motherhood, staring into that mirror with total honesty and acceptance of the brutal truth, I see myself as a person who makes a *lot* of mistakes.

But it's okay, because that's why God invented apologies. In fact, Jewish tradition has a whole practice specifically focused on what to do when we mess up. It's called *teshuvah*, which literally means "return."

A beautiful and central part of Jewish practice, teshuvah is a sort of karmic reset. It begins with apologizing, but it doesn't end there; you also have to repair any damage you've done, change your behavior, and act differently the next time you find yourself in a similar situation.

Teshuvah is a powerful spiritual technology, a way to deal with the fact that we hurt each other without meaning to and need to find our way back to each other.

This practice is front and center during the ten-day period between Rosh Hashanah and Yom Kippur. Each fall, as we celebrate the New Year, we try to repair any damage we did the previous year and then reorient ourselves for the next.

Taking ten days to reset and repair is transformative. But as our tradition teaches, and as every parent knows, apologizing isn't just for the High Holy Days.

We need it every day. Multiple times a day. Sometimes, multiple times an hour.

Perhaps this is why, according to the Talmud, God actually created teshuvah before creating the world. Before light and dark, before the firmament and the ocean, before animals and people. The world itself is grounded in the practice of teshuvah, in its ability to repair our mistakes, to heal, to move forward.

Instead of shaming us for our shortcomings, or hoping that one day we'll transcend our flaws, this fundamental vision of teshuvah instead grants us a way to repair the damage we are certain to do just by virtue of being human.

The need to start over, to recalibrate, is a basic part of human existence. And perhaps it's part of divine existence too; there's a mystical tradition that God creates the whole world anew every single day. Often this concept is understood metaphorically: a reminder to look around us and notice just how miraculous the world is. But some medieval kabbalists understood it as a literal truth.

In this mystical worldview, God is literally creating the world anew each day. It's a state of "perpetual creation," a pulsing stream of energy that never stops flowing from *ayin* (nothingness) to *yeish* (existence). If God stopped this flow of creation for even just a moment, the world would literally disappear. But God never stops; the world keeps going, reborn and recreated—second after second, miracle after miracle.

This idea of constant flow, perpetual creation, resonates with my life right now, as I watch my kids' warp-speed growth. I watch their bodies sprout from rotund toddler-pushing-a-lawnmower-toy to leggy elementary-schooler-on-a-big-kid-trampoline; I watch their obsessions shift from Duplos to complicated superhero Lego structures; I watch their screen time migrate from squeaky-voiced cartoons to aspirational-tween TV shows.

And as they change, our relationships, too, are constantly being recreated. I marvel at how much room there is for us to grow together into places I can't even imagine yet.

The world is constantly being created, and so is teshuvah. Always available, always ready for us to step into it—as parents and as people. We can always apologize and change our ways. We can always reconnect.

And then we jump back into the unceasing flow of new creation, and relax knowing that we don't have to create the world—we just have to return to it, over and over.

64
Goodbye, Baby Years

As we leave the early stages of our parenting journey, others are just beginning the journey. It's someone else's turn now.

We talk a lot about kid benchmarks and parenting milestones: first word, first steps, first day of school. But there's one milestone we don't usually talk about: the moment we decide we're done having babies.

Sometimes, this is a voluntary decision. Sometimes it comes because of outside forces, whether physical, financial, or emotional. Often it's a complex combination of external and internal forces, negotiations, and conversations with partners or family or oneself.

And just as there are many ways we reach this milestone, there's a wide range of ways we feel in response. Some of my friends report feeling a simple sense of relief and fulfillment when they pronounce, "We're done!" Others are surprised at the deep feeling of loss that accompanies this decision.

As for me, as the oldest of three sisters, I grew up feeling like three was the number that made a family complete. If you'd asked me how many kids I wanted, I would have said three. That number felt like the perfect balance of chaos and manageability: big enough to be your own little crew, small enough to fit in a sedan.

My husband, Aaron, however, felt strongly that two was where he wanted to stop.

He knew I had always wanted three, but the truth was, I wasn't really in a position to argue too strongly for that number.

Since we lived across the country from family, there was no wiggle room; if one of us got a stomach flu, it threw our entire world into crisis mode. And even more importantly, my work as a musician and teacher meant that I traveled frequently. Aaron took great care of our kids when I was away, but it wouldn't have been right to throw another baby at him—and I loved my work and knew that giving it up would be terrible for everyone.

It just wouldn't be right for me to insist on another baby, much as I wanted one.

Every day for years, I told Aaron, "I know we've decided, but I want you to know that I still want that third baby." Aaron would look into my eyes and say, "I'm sorry, I know."

And that was enough. I desperately wanted that third child, but I also loved our family as it was. In my heart, I knew: this was one of those compromises that adults make when faced with reality.

Still, if I'm being honest, I can't help feeling a little twist in my heart when I see a mom with three kids. And if I wake up feeling slightly nauseous on a random morning, a tiny part of me wonders if maybe, just maybe, my husband's vasectomy was one of those "oops" ones. And when Sylvia says she wishes she had a little sister, I say, "I know what you mean."

Even though our decision is final, naming this feeling of loss helps me to relax around it rather than fight it. At this point, Aaron is not at all surprised when I randomly walk into the kitchen and say, "I really want another baby." He knows I'm not actually asking for a reversal surgery—I'm just telling him how I feel.

Realizing that I'm not alone has also been helpful. Since I've started opening up about this, I've met many parents who feel the same way, regardless of how many kids they already have. I know a mom of six who wrote a beautiful post about her difficult decision not to have a seventh. Reading her words helped me realize: if we mothers can still feel an absence after six kids, maybe that feeling is not a problem to solve, but just part of the process.

And the flip side of this feeling of absence is knowing there's space in my heart to take care of another child, another teenager, another person. When I was in high school, and my best friend ran away from home, my parents took him in for a while (after calling his family to make sure they knew he was safe). I trust that when it's time, that person will find me, and I'll be ready to welcome them.

Everything ends: the baby years, the toddler years, the elementary school years, the years of having kids at home. As we leave the early stages of our parenting journey, others are just beginning the journey. It's someone else's turn.

Somewhere, right now, someone is making the momentous decision to become a parent, someone is sitting on the toilet looking wide-eyed at a little plus sign, someone is in labor, someone is signing foster or adoption papers, someone is watching their baby take her first steps.

For a while, that someone was us. We were Mama, or Mommy, or Dad, or Nopa, or Baba: Whatever our kids called us, it was an all-consuming, starring role. It was demanding and rewarding and exhausting and exhilarating and boring, all at once.

Sometimes it felt like we couldn't go on for another moment, and sometimes it felt like we could do this forever, and often it was a combination of the two. And then, seemingly overnight, it was over.

It's all part of the mystery of parenthood. The way time expands and contracts. One day we have to wake up every two hours, when all we want to do is sleep. Soon enough, we'll have to let go when all we want to do is hold on.

We're all on this ride together—us, our kids, our ancestors, our descendants. We all grow up, together.

65

Every Ending Contains a Beginning

Goodbye and hello are the refrain of parenting. We continually let go of one mode of existence to welcome another.

When Sylvia turned two, we could tell she was ready to transition from her bedtime bottle of milk to a cup.

To prepare her, we told her we were going to say, "Goodbye, bottle—hello, cup." She loved saying it with us: "Goodbye, bottle—hello, cup." It seemed to help her understand what was happening. And it helped me understand too.

Goodbye and hello are the refrain of parenting. From pregnancy to childbirth to the daily work of raising kids, we continually let go of one mode of existence to welcome another. Goodbye, dreamy newborn—hello, inquisitive six-month-old. Goodbye, sweet one-year-old—hello, stomping toddler. And so it goes.

And as it does so often, the Torah mirrors this as well. In its final chapters, we say goodbye to the years the Israelites have spent wandering in the desert, their "childhood," and we also say goodbye to Moses himself, their leader.

Moses prepares for his death by blessing those who have come before him. Each of the tribes descends from one of Jacob's sons—Reuben, Simeon, Levi, Judah, etc.—and Moses addresses each tribe by the name of that original ancestor. Even though he was born hundreds of years after these ancestors died, Moses has preserved their stories: who was quick to anger, who was good at fishing, who was especially faithful.

I'm touched by the care Moses takes in recalling these brothers he never met. Their long-ago actions—fathering the twelve tribes, going down to Egypt, making peace with their brother Joseph— were what made Moses's extraordinary life possible. He honors this by invoking their names as he blesses their descendants.

The world Moses knew is unimaginably different from our modern lives. But so much remains the same. Babies are born, they grow up and have babies of their own, and they pass away and leave the earth to their unknown great-great-grandchildren. That's what happens with Moses as the Torah draws to a close. And if you zoom out far enough, you can see that happening to all of us, right now.

In our extreme close-up experience of parenting young kids, time looks like a big, slow mess of spills, snuggles, tantrums, dances, three a.m. nursing sessions, birthdays, childcare, delighted squeals on the tire swing, and hour-long walks around the block.

But if we pull back a bit we see a very different picture, a great, slowly turning wheel, a procession of lifetimes. Adam and Eve, Abraham and Sarah, the twelve tribes, Moses, the many generations that came after him, our great-grandparents, us, our kids, and their great-grandchildren, whom we'll never know.

When we finish the Torah, we begin reading it all over again. We are all part of this slowly turning wheel, this procession of lifetimes. We hop on, we hop off, but the cycle continues.

66

We Will Return to Each Other

Sooner or later, our kids grow out of being little kids, and we grow out of being parents of little kids.

Dear Mama,

When I was growing up, my mother had a little cross-stitch hanging on the wall that read, "Families are for growing up in, going away from, and coming back to."

As a teenager, I understood the first two phrases, but I couldn't wrap my mind around the last part. I loved my family, but I couldn't wait to set out on my own. I knew that one day I'd want a family of my own too—but I thought that would be a continuation of the second phrase in the cross-stitch, growing "away from" my family of origin.

But as I grew older and became a parent myself, I began remembering childhood images of my grandmother. I began to see myself as my parents' daughter in a new way, and to feel the hovering presence of mothers going back many generations. I realized that for me, having kids *was* coming back.

Every family of origin is different. It's my great good fortune that I happened to be born into a healthy, supportive one, one that is safe for me to return to. For some of us, it's healthier to return with clear boundaries in place, or to return to chosen family instead of birth family. Still, there is this sense, this need, to fold back into a safe space that nurtures you.

Growing up, going away, coming back. These simple words contain some deep wisdom, and they remind me of a concept in Jewish tradition. When we complete a particular course of study—a book of the Talmud, say, or reading through the entire Torah, or even a deep dive into a single chapter—we celebrate with a *siyum*, which literally means "finishing."

A siyum is a ritual celebration of completion. We set out on a project, we stuck with it, and we made it to the end. And so we have a little party.

But of course, a siyum is not *really* the end. Because stories—and life—may appear linear, but they are also cyclical. Our sacred texts were originally written down as scrolls, not books. We wind them, each chapter leading on to the next, and then we wind them back to the beginning and start again.

Raising kids, too, is both cyclical and linear. The phrase "two steps forward, one step back" haunted me during my kids' early years. Just when I thought my toddler had finally grown out of a certain behavior, it would pop up again (the phrase "sleep regression" still strikes terror into my heart).

And yet, as they grow older, most kids *do* need us less and less. That helpless little bundle of human potential we hold in the early days and months grows into the glorious, full person they are meant to be.

Little by little, they learn to tie their own shoes, wash their own dishes, be kind to those around them, take good care of themselves, and keep learning and growing. Perhaps they'll even become parents one day. And yet every parent of adults assures me that I'll never stop being a parent—emotionally, financially, spiritually—no matter how old my kids get.

There is a traditional Aramaic phrase we recite at a siyum. It's sweet and somewhat surprising, in that we speak directly to the text we have just finished studying. "*Hadran alach*," we say. "We will return to you."

Learning our holy texts, like parenting, is never-ending. There are always deeper insights to realize, new perspectives to uncover.

As my mother's cross-stitch might put it: our stories and texts are for growing up in, leaving, and coming back to.

Mystical Judaism believes in reincarnation, which is called *gilgul*. This comes from the Hebrew word *l'galgeil*, meaning "to roll." The idea is that our souls, like a wheel, recur over, and over, and over again.

Perhaps we literally come back as other people, or perhaps we are just connected to our ancestors, to all who have gone before and all who will come later.

Sooner or later, it happens to all of us: our kids grow out of being little kids, and we grow out of being parents of little kids. We've studied that book, of baby life and early childhood; we've been thrown up on and screamed at, had our hair patted by tiny sticky hands and our shoulders hugged by chunky little arms.

"Hadran alach," we say as the chapter ends; *we will return to you.* The truth is, we're not really leaving at all. We're just moving down the conveyor belt along with our kids, continuing to do what we've done from the beginning of this journey: loving the human in front of us as they grow and change.

And yet there *is* a sense of completion as we reach the end of early childhood, this holy book of human learning, and it's worth marking with a *siyum*. Not that we know everything about it—far from it!—but that we have passed through this cycle, this time around. And now we are on to other challenges, other journeys, other adventures.

We say it together, as we leave the early years of parenting and move on to whatever comes next. Hadran alach, our little ones, rapidly turning into big kids before our eyes. Hadran alach, our own years immersed in early parenthood—this passage, this privilege, this sacred initiation.

Now we begin the next chapter in the scroll of our own family story. Now it's our children's turn to fulfill the prophecy of that cross-stitch: to grow up, to go away from us, and if we're very lucky, to come back.

Acknowledgments

D eep gratitude to my family and friends, and to the many midwives and doulas of this project.

To Deborah Kolben, Molly Tolsky, and Kveller, for hosting my year-long series of weekly Torah portion commentary through the eyes of a new parent, which grew into this book. A special shout-out to Molly for her capable and compassionate editing during the Kveller days. Thanks also to David Suissa at the Los Angeles *Jewish Journal*, where some of these essays first appeared.

To Behrman House—especially David Behrman, Vicki Weber, and Dena Neusner—thank you for believing in this book and making it a reality. Gratitude to Tzivia MacLeod for the absolutely excellent editing. And also to the Covenant Foundation, especially Harlene Winnick Appelman and Joni Blinderman Levine, the only people who can get me to perform at breakfast, which is where I met David.

I'm forever grateful to my teachers and professors at the Pardes Institute of Jewish Studies and the Jewish Theological Seminary. Also to my b'nei mitzvah students and their families. To the rabbis and sages of our tradition, and to my ancestors for passing this heritage down. And to the countless Jewish mothers, healers, and mystics over the millennia. Though their wisdom was often left out of the written canon, it lives in us still.

For time and space, thanks to Alyssa Isenstein Krueger for the cat-sitting "residency," and to Jake Marmer and the Bronfman Youth Fellowship for the writing-and-teaching residency at Isabella Freedman. (And to Aaron for taking care of the kids while I wrote about taking care of the kids.)

Writer beloveds! Thanks to Vanessa Hua for being my forever conference spouse and giving me the idea to make a necklace out of many individual beads; this book wouldn't exist without you. To Rebecca Clarren for all the writerly walks and talks (and the mikvah story). To Jesse Lichtenstein, David Naimon, Chrys Tobey, and Vandoren Wheeler. And to Matt Walker for the backyard Mishnah chavruta.

Thanks to my mom friends, old and new; you know who you are. I'd be lost without you. Thanks to Uriah Boyd, Sarah Broderick, Jane Gottesman, and Danielle Carver for help and support on this project. And thanks to everyone whose stories are contained or alluded to in this book; I hope I did them justice.

Eternal gratitude to my own parents, Karen and Peter Rabins, for being the best mother and father I could possibly imagine. The rabbis are right—I'll never be able to thank you enough. Extra thanks to you for proofreading, Mom.

To Aaron Hartman, husband and father extraordinaire: thank you for walking this path with me, being such an amazing dad to our kids, and loving me through it all. There's no one else I'd rather be on this wild ride with.

To Sylvia and Elijah, my beloveds, my big-kids-already, my teachers. Thank you for letting me write about our life together. I love you forever.

Bibliography

Almond, Barbara. "Maternal Ambivalence: The Dilemma of Modern Parenting." *Psychology Today* (blog), September 16, 2010. https://www.psychologytoday.com/intl/blog/maternal-ambivalence/201009/maternal-ambivalence.

Ames, Louise Bates. *Your Two-Year-Old*. New York: Dell, 1976.

Behrendt, Greg, and Liz Tuccillo. *He's Just Not That into You*. New York: Gallery Books, 2006.

di Prima, Diane. *Memoirs of a Beatnik*. New York: Penguin Books, 1998.

Egan, Kerry. *On Living*. New York: Riverhead Books, 2016.

Nachman, Rebbe. *Likutey Moharan*. Translated by Moshe Mykoff and Symchah Bergman. Jerusalem: Breslov Research Institute, 1986.

Naphtali, Sarah. *Buddhism for Mothers of Young Children*. Crows Nest, Australia: Allen & Unwin, 2009.

Sacks, Rabbi Jonathan. *Covenant & Conversation: A Weekly Reading of the Jewish Bible, Exodus: The Book of Redemption*. Jerusalem: Maggid Books, 2010.

Schnarch, David. *Passionate Marriage: Keeping Love and Intimacy Alive in Committed Relationships*. New York: W. W. Norton, 1997.

Solnit, Rebecca. *A Field Guide to Getting Lost*. New York: Penguin Random House, 2006.